THE JOY COMPASS

8 ways to find lasting happiness, gratitude & optimism in the present moment

DONALD ALTMAN, MA, LPC

New Harbinger Publications, Inc.

Distributed in Canada by Raincoast Books

New Harbinger Publications, Inc.
5674 Shattuck Avenue
Oakland, CA 94609
www.newharbinger.com

Acquired by Jess O'Brien; Cover design by Amy Shoup;
Edited by Nelda Street; Text design by Tracy Carlson

Library of Congress Cataloging-in-Publication Data

Altman, Don, 1950-
The joy compass : eight ways to find lasting happiness, gratitude, and optimism in the present moment / Donald Altman ; foreword by Robert Biswas-Diener.
p. cm.
Includes bibliographical references.
ISBN 978-1-60882-283-6 (pbk. : alk. paper) -- ISBN 978-1-60882-284-3 (pdf e-book) -- ISBN 978-1-60882-285-0 (epub)
1. Happiness. 2. Gratitude. 3. Optimism. 4. Mind and body. I. Title.
BF575.H27.A448 2012
158--dc23

2012015223

Printed in the United States of America

14 13 12 10 9 8 7 6 5 4 3 2 1 First printing

If you have this book in your hands you are about to make an exponential leap orward in your own personal evolution. Altman's compassionate, sturdy voice gen-ly guides you through seemingly disparate pieces of your internal landscape back o your center, from which self-reliance, self-worth, empathy, and a renewed sense of your innate natural joy can abound. This is a calming and inspirational manual or restructuring any faltering emotional system; an exploration of this book may esult in effervescent joy and unbridled contentment."

—Christopher Kennedy Lawford, goodwill ambassador to the United Nations, CEO of Recover to Live and Global Recovery Initiative, global speaker on recovery, and best-selling author of *Moments of Clarity* and *Symptoms of Withdrawal*

The most important discovery that human beings can make is the discovery that hey can change their state of mind from negative to positive. We do not have to e victims of our minds and its moods. In this book Donald Altman describes eight imple ways (tested and proven by research) that we all can become more joyful and at ease in our lives. It's just what the doctor prescribed—free happiness medi-cine! Why don't you try it?"

—Jan Chozen Bays, MD, pediatrician and Zen *rōshi* (teacher), and author of *Mindful Eating: A Guide to Rediscovering a Healthy and Joyful Relationship with Food* and *How to Train a Wild Elephant: And Other Adventures in Mindfulness*

"*The Joy Compass* is a refreshingly user-friendly manual that nimbly demonstrates Donald Altman's decades of expert experience teaching practical techniques of applied mindfulness. This potent little book provides extremely timely advice for a stressed-out society!"

—Jeffrey M. Schwartz, MD, coauthor of *You Are Not Your Brain*

"*The Joy Compass* presents invaluable insights and exercises for training yourself to be more present, lucid, and filled with joy—even during life's most ordinary moments. It is a must-read for anybody who is serious about developing present-moment awareness, simple happiness, and freedom from anxiety and depression. Use it just like a sailor uses a real compass—as a guide into the calm joy of sunny skies and quiet seas."

—Tobin Blake, author of *Everyday Meditation: 100 Daily Meditations for Health, Stress Relief, and Everyday Joy*

"What a refreshing guide to rejuvenation and self-discovery. Donald Altman's new book, *The Joy Compass*, provides eight strategies that will open your mind to possibilities you may never have considered. This book is a must-read for all who are seeking mental enrichment in ways that are as fun to read as they are perceptive."

—John Baldoni, author of *Lead with Purpose: Giving Your Organization a Reason to Believe in Itself*

"Study after study shows that people who are happy and optimistic are also healthier and live longer—and now Donald Altman has given us a wonderfully practical guide to achieving the very emotions and attitudes that ensure good health. Highly recommended!"

—Bill Gottlieb, CHC, author of *Alternative Cures*

"Donald Altman's books are always full of creativity, kindness and wisdom. This former Buddhist monk is a monastery onto himself, growing a virtual sangha of readers around the ancient meme of joy and presence. *The Joy Compass* is perhaps Altman's most brilliant metaphor to date. Life is a pursuit of well-being, and learning to pay attention to this body/mind compass of joy within us is the ultimate skill of living. With engineering precision, Altman introduces the know-how of attention-training and intention-training and then walks you through a variety of life-applications. The result? A comprehensive map to well-being, with an effective built-in compass to guide your journey!"

—Pavel Somov, PhD, author of *Eating the Moment*, *The Lotus Effect*, and *Reinventing the Meal*

"Don't be fooled, *The Joy Compass* is not the latest 'feel good' book—though it certainly will point the way to living a life of mindfulness, purpose and fulfillment. Donald Altman's 'compass' comes from his years of practicing in his own life what he teaches in this book and facilitates for his clients and students. He describes the various paths and practices it takes to live life as a creator, rather than a victim to all the forces in the world that conspire to steer us away from a life of choices and vitality. His simple—yet profound—writing rhythm offers 'content, practice, and reflection.' This is the 'CPR' our modern life needs for resuscitation!"

—David Emerald, co-founder of the Bainbridge Leadership Center and author of *The Power of TED (The Empowerment Dynamic)* and co-author of *TED for Diabetes: A Health Empowerment Story*

Contents

Acknowledgments

My deepest gratitude extends to all those who have dedicated themselves to sharing with others the teachings of peace and mindfulness. I thank my late teacher, the Venerable U. Silananda, who was a dedicated mindfulness guide for so many; Ashin Thitzana, a spiritual friend and monk brother whose laughter brings joy to many; U. Thondara and the monks and community of the Burma Buddhist Monastery; Randy Fitzgerald, a friend and writer whose enthusiasm and generous sharing of ideas and resources helped shape this book; Greg Crosby, a friend whose knowledge of mythology helped enhance these pages; Robert Biswas-Diener, a friend and happiness researcher, who was kind enough to share his special wisdom and insights in the foreword; John Kuzma, a friend whose generous spirit helped usher this book forward; fellow board members of the Center for Mindful Eating, for bringing joy into the world through an enlightened awareness of food and eating; Bill Gladstone, my agent, for passionately supporting this book; Jess O'Brien and Nicola Skidmore, my editors, who shepherded this work by contributing numerous wonderful ideas and insights, and all of the people at New Harbinger who had a role in helping make this book possible; and copyeditor Nelda Street, for her keen editorial talents.

Finally, this book would not have been possible without so many others—guides, friends, colleagues, clients, acquaintances, students, and so on—who have served daily as my gifted and courageous teachers in exploring and practicing joy. I am deeply indebted to my brother and sister, Jim and Cynthia, for their kind and generous spirit, and to my parents, Barbara and Norman, for the lessons and kindness they have offered me. May all beings experience the grace and lightness of joy; may we step onto this peaceful, humble, sustainable path together, continuing to coawaken and coheal in each unfolding moment.

Foreword

Let's clear this up at the outset: I am a scientist. That means that I tend to think about things in empirical terms. I like proof. I privilege evidence. I place a premium on things I can taste, touch, and see. This does not mean that I doubt the existence of a higher power or dismiss anything that has not yet been proven. Indeed, I like theories as well as facts. I just want to make it clear that my natural tendency is to talk about physiology rather than energy, emotional states rather than vibrations, and facts rather than coincidences. This is—I suppose—my long-winded way of saying that when it comes to the topic of mindfulness, I was long content to leave the subject to Buddhists and others with a head for such things. In fact, I think I can be honest in saying that I basically dismissed mindfulness techniques as a spiritual niche with little relevance to my own life.

What's more, I had solid evidence that I did not even need mindfulness. I knew myself to be a person who was particularly aware of his surroundings—a guy who often took the time to savor successes and who felt self-aware. Boy, was I wrong! I have come to realize that the story I was telling myself—that I was intensely aware of my moment-to-moment surroundings—was, ironically, a narrative that existed up in my head and was divorced from the realities of daily existence. One of the people I credit with this insight is Donald Altman. Donald is a therapist and a mindfulness practitioner and is possessed of a deep reservoir of charitable intention for his fellow human. Donald and I meet a few times a year to have coffee and to chat, and it was during these meetings that he opened my eyes to the power of mindfulness. Donald is not a preacher, and he was not looking to convert me. It was just that his centered, soft-spoken manner and emotional honesty were so admirable that I felt compelled to take a deeper look.

In many ways I envy you, the reader, in that you hold in your hands a book that contains practical and powerful tools for achieving the things that are truly important in life: happiness, hope, and a sense of peace. At every turn, Altman provides very practical advice and easy-to-conduct exercises. They are alternately playful, insightful, quick, fun, and reflective. After using his book for only two chapters, I found myself changing my attitudes toward mindfulness. I loved starting with the "puppy mind" exercise and allowed myself to wander all over my house as my interest and whimsy carried me. It felt silly and wonderful, and it also illustrated how clearly our thoughts can be both within and outside our control. I especially liked the bodily sensation exercises—perhaps because I am an empiricist! It is deceptive how paying attention to your bodily sensation—the pressure on your feet as you stand or the mild stiffness in your neck—can bring you out of the running commentary of your head and into the real world.

Perhaps my favorite of all of Altman's examples was his point that we frequently hold silent conversations with other people in our heads. I know I have had countless arguments (and won almost all of them!) long after the real-world fight has finished. I know I have offered expert commentary to my friends on how they ought to raise their children or decorate their houses—all in my own head, of course. I might even have prepared an Academy Award acceptance speech or two. The point here is that we spend an awful lot of time living in the remote penthouse of the mind when the real action of life is down on the street level. Altman acts as an elevator operator, taking us where we most need to go. And for that, we should thank him.

—Robert Biswas-Diener, DrPhilos
Portland, Oregon

Introduction

Have you ever known anyone with the extraordinarily fortuitous capability to tune in to joy and other positive mental states on a consistent basis? Even when confronted by life's many challenges, such individuals are able to maintain a sense of equanimity, composure, and poise. What's more, they seem to tap into these qualities with ease and effortlessness. You are not alone if you find yourself asking questions like: How do they do it? Why does it seem so easy for them? Are they just wired differently from the rest of us?

In these pages you will discover a valuable secret: joyful states of mind and well-being are not reserved for a privileged few, but available and accessible to all. Perhaps most important, being in a state of joy is a learned skill, not an innate ability. This is accomplished by using your personal joy compass: an internal, portable navigational guide activated through moment-to-moment awareness. This personal compass points you toward sublime states of being when you need them most: whenever you are feeling down, stuck, or confronted by anxiety-provoking stressors, or whenever you want to feel good, as well as more energized, enthusiastic, and positive about life. Just as the magnetized needle in a compass naturally aligns with the earth's magnetic field to help you find your way, the mindfulness pathways explored in *The Joy Compass* continually point you toward true joy.

While mindfulness has been understood in a broad number of ways, I like to view it as the possibility of awakening (to joy and other positive mood states) and the awakening of possibility. With mindfulness, you bring a sense of openness and acceptance to what is happening in this moment through the body, the mind, and the spirit. To do so opens a world of possibility where you can find joy.

To make your joy compass fully operational, you will first need to calibrate and align your mental tools of awareness—namely, attention and intention. Once they are aligned, attention and intention, skillfully used, let you interact with your internal world of thoughts and feelings—as well as the external world of people, places, and things—in a centering, calming, and positive way. The result of this mental calibration process is that you actually rewire the brain so that it is ready to access joy. The latest brain science, for example, reveals that your brain gets wired depending on the joyful or nonjoyful choices you make. This is both sobering and promising news. Consider the following two personal choices: spending time in isolation while practicing an addictive and unproductive behavior, or intentionally engaging in pleasant and productive activities with a supportive social network. Choosing either one of these options affects the brain—and your level of joy—in profound ways.

Fortunately, *The Joy Compass* will give you the mindfulness skills required to make new and beneficial choices with greater awareness and intentionality. When you properly align attention and intention, you will discover that focusing on joy is not an accident, but a powerful choice that is within your control. In addition, this new alignment overcomes the brain's innate "negativity bias," the tendency to look for any danger or threat to survival—no matter how small. Basically the brain is saying, "It's safer to suck all the joy out of this moment than to take the chance of encountering that one danger that could end my life if I'm not careful!" That's why traumatic events and negative memories can act as powerful filters that block out the present moment—particularly, joyful moments. The brain's self-protection circuitry will still be there when you need it, but your new default setting will be joy. Does this mean that you will never again experience unhappiness, sadness, or other upsetting emotions? That's a nice idea, but the truth is that there is pain in life. Joy is not an instant, magical elixir that erases the truth of pain and loss. Tuning in to joy doesn't mean that you will escape the hardships of old age or the sadness that comes from losing loved ones. It doesn't mean that your boss will suddenly grow a heart of gold (or even just a heart) and give you that well-deserved raise. Those frustrating traffic jams aren't going to miraculously disappear. That dreary and annoying winter weather won't suddenly give way to sunshine (just as it won't stop raining in Portland, where I live).

What having a working joy compass does mean is that *you* can decide how to respond by skillfully directing your awareness. I'm not saying that you should ignore negative emotions and painful experiences—or that you will never again experience depression or anxiety. There is often something important to be learned from the pain that life gives us.

Rather than use up an incredible amount of energy on rejecting or pushing away uncomfortable feelings, it is more empowering to be present with the conditions in your life. When I was a Buddhist monk, I learned how to use mindfulness as a way to stay balanced, accepting, and flexible with whatever life brings. Today, as a practicing psychotherapist, I use mindfulness concepts to help people shift toward positive states of awareness. The point is that while you can't wave a magic wand to make pain go away, your joy compass can help you counterbalance pain so that you can move forward instead of getting stuck and feeling hopeless, and this is no small thing.

I remember the first time that Paul, a fifty-three-year-old office manager, stepped into my office. Deep furrows contorted his brow as he told me that constant layoffs at his workplace produced so much worry and concern that he secretly cried most days at work. Many of Paul's coworkers had already lost their jobs because of downsizing, and the once-happy office had become filled with fear and anger. Instead of being his unflappable self—always sharing a laugh or a story with others—Paul retreated to his office, waiting for the inevitable layoff. Meanwhile, his adult daughter moved back home because of debt and the loss of her own job. An honorable and caring father, he decided to bail his daughter out of debt using his own savings. This meant that instead of preparing for his golden years, he and his wife now needed to work well into their sixties. Filled with uncertainty about the future, Paul had fallen into a deep depression.

Slowly, Paul began to locate joy and hope in his life. He started by reconnecting with others at his workplace. I encouraged him to share his feelings with people he trusted. Later, I instructed Paul on how to reduce stress and find joy—using the methods in this book. Then one day, Paul sat down, looking more relieved than I had ever seen him. He flashed a smile and said, "I played around with different joy practices this week. During my break, I practiced the breathing to reduce stress. Then I went outside and was looking at ivy that was growing up a tree trunk. I could see that the fern had been cut back at one point but had started to grow again. Suddenly, I realized that all of life goes in cycles, and I felt this sense of relief. Everything has a season, even a job. I knew that if I got laid off, I would find a way to continue and grow again—just like that plant." Paul soon got another position that was more challenging. But he liked and appreciated the new job, as well as the thought of finding joy in his work.

As Paul's story illustrates, life contains both the light and the darkness. If you have only one or the other, you may be missing out on the perfectly messy and holistic nature of all of life that is before you right now. By using your personal joy compass, you can find balance while living with your negative emotions, rather than stamp them out as if they were something ugly and unwarranted. As you learn to access joy, you may find that negative emotions do not pull on you as strongly. You might also discover that you more readily can switch to joy rather than dwell and ruminate endlessly on life's inevitable pain—which is really a way to heap on extra (and optional) helpings of suffering.

Finally, and perhaps most important, you may begin to grasp that joy is not an external thing that is located "out there." Going back to its early thirteenth-century roots, the word "joy" refers to an expression of positive emotion through rejoicing. Rather than being an external object, joy is a state of moment-to-moment being and experiencing. Advertisers, for example, want you to believe that joy and satisfaction are found by buying their products. The implication is that you are incomplete and that the inadequacies that cause your unhappiness can be remedied only through getting the right car, job, relationship, clothing, cosmetics, and so on. The result of this narrow approach, however, is that you grow conditioned to seek joy outside of yourself.

As you align with joy and practice using your joy compass, you will gain a deeper understanding and appreciation of the real underpinnings of sustainable joy and how to access it through the wise blending of attention, mental states, and the environment. And, because the brain learns through experience, these pages are filled with exercises and practices designed to establish a new neurocircuitry of joy.

To help you navigate the journey to joy, *The Joy Compass* consists of three parts. Part 1, "Developing Attention and Intention," comprises two chapters that are primers for understanding that your thoughts are not necessarily facts. This part of the book will give you the tools to take control over where and how you place your attention.

Part 2, "Mindfulness Pathways to Joy and Positive Moods," details mindfulness pathways for creating and sustaining joy. Each of its eight chapters focuses on a unique mindfulness pathway that acts as a compass for locating joy, from the powerful biochemistry of laughter to the mood-shifting ability of gratitude.

In the back of the book, "Resources for Continuing Your Journey to Joy" investigates how coming to the end of locating joy is really the beginning. It is a valuable resource guide that lists various websites that link to joy.

My hope is that you will find the joy that has always been waiting for you. And as your joy compass more frequently points you toward joy in its many forms, don't be surprised if others start to notice the difference. I know of a nurse, for example, whose life took a drastic turn after she embraced gratitude as a means to finding joy. Whereas before she was easily wound up, irritated, and moody, she was now easygoing, smiling, and always available to assist others. She told me that on more than one occasion, a coworker had come up to her and said, "Are you on antidepressants? You are so much happier than you used to be!"

"No, I'm not on antidepressants," she answered. "I'm on gratitude, and the view is a whole lot better from here."

Wherever life leads you, may your joy compass guide you to a place of greater peace, harmony, and joy.

PART 1

Developing Attention & Intention

CHAPTER 1

Becoming Friends with Your Mind and Body

You can use your joy compass whenever you feel lost or negative, or feel as if you have wandered off the path of happiness and fulfillment. This joy compass, however, can work only when you are able to direct your thoughts and your attention. By mastering awareness, you gain the means to befriend that most complex and multilayered universe that lies within: the human mind.

Can you think of an example in which your inability to focus or think clearly adversely affected your life? If you normally focus on the negative during stressful times, it may surprise you to know that you have a choice. Skillfully using the mind's faculty of attention can not only make life more tolerable, but also enhance it with greater joy, meaning, and hope.

One wonderful illustration of the power of attention can be found in the life of the brilliant mathematician and economist John Nash, whose struggles were chronicled in the film A

Beautiful Mind (Goldsman and Nasar 2001). Nash was tormented by delusions that were so real that they skewed his reality and made daily living extremely hard. Eventually, he came to recognize that his mind was not always playing fair, because it often depicted illusion—actually, delusion—as fact. Near the end of the film, Nash is asked if the imaginary individuals who were part of his psyche are still with him. Nash pauses and then wisely answers that although he still sees these individuals, he chooses to ignore them. In his own way, Nash learned the essential lesson that thoughts in the mind—even the most compelling and persistent ones—are not necessarily truth. While John Nash's story is an extreme one, it points out what can happen when you take your own thoughts too seriously.

The thing is, we all have the tendency to take *our* thoughts more seriously than we would the thoughts of another because they come from within our own heads! While this is a natural tendency, it doesn't need to be an enduring one.

Are you ready to explore your own inner world of thoughts? As you take on the experiences that follow, keep in mind that your thoughts are not necessarily facts—no matter how critical the thoughts might be. You can observe them in a neutral way, just as a detective looks for clues.

What's Rattling Around in There?

The good news is that your brain is already wired to attain mindful awareness. This ability to know what you are thinking and feeling is centered in the part of the brain located just behind your forehead and eyes—known as the *prefrontal cortex*. When you align your awareness, you will be activating and lighting up the circuits in this part of the brain. The more you turn on these circuits, the easier it becomes to notice thoughts in a more neutral and impartial way so that you can examine them more easily.

Let's do a little practice to begin training and taming your mind's attention. I like to call this "training the puppy mind," because the mind is like an untrained puppy with its favorite toys that it likes to grab onto and vigorously shake, and that it never tires of running after. It takes a lot of training and consistency to teach a puppy to come when you call its name, as well as to get it to sit and heel at your side as you walk. This takes many repetitions and a lot of time. So, too, with puppy mind.

Practice: Training the Puppy Mind

For the next three minutes, get up and walk around the room or space that you are in. Do this without any particular goal in mind. Go wherever or do whatever attracts your attention. If you need to attend to a task you've been thinking about, go and do that. When time is up, come back to the book, with a pad of paper and a pencil.

Congratulations on letting your puppy mind wander free. Now, using the pad of paper, try to track all the places your puppy mind visited when you let it run free for those three minutes.

Write down as many thoughts as you can recall. Don't worry if there are some (or many) that you can't quite put your finger on. Thoughts often fall into the following categories. Use this list to jog your memory of thoughts you engaged in over those three minutes:

- Thoughts about the future
- Thoughts or memories related to the past
- Thoughts about potential conversations with others
- Thoughts related to physical sensations, such as hunger, craving, pain, and so on
- Fantasies that provide a feeling of pleasure or escape

Reflections on Training the Puppy Mind

What was it like to try to pinpoint all the thoughts that you have bouncing around in your head? Don't judge yourself harshly if you couldn't remember all your thoughts. Also, don't be critical if your thoughts were not what you thought or hoped they would be. Just know that as you move forward, you will become more proficient at recognizing your thoughts, as well as determining what you would like your well-trained mental puppy to pay attention to. Congratulations on taking this important first step!

Catching Your Mind Whispers

As a psychotherapist, I have frequently worked with clients who were unceremoniously yanked around by their thoughts. Often, they were stuck in a habit or addiction that caused untold grief and guilt. One such person, Rodney, was a successful salesman who spent hours each day surfing for pornography online—to the dismay and sadness of his wife. When asked if he had a plan to make changes, he answered yes. But when his wife asked what that plan was, Rodney was confused. "I don't know," he answered, adding, "I think I'm thinking about it." Although Rodney believed he was thinking about it, he really didn't know the contents of his own mind. Rodney's mind was stuck in the sticky spider web of the Internet. He was no longer in charge of his own attention.

Practice: Writing and Riding the Flow

This practice consists of spending five minutes just writing with no agenda. It serves the purpose of letting you become friends with the ever-changing torrent of mental events—memories, thoughts, fantasies, opinions, worries, desires, and so on—that comprise mind. If you feel some fear, reticence, or resistance to doing this exercise, that's normal. Just know that you can always shred or burn your "Writing and Riding the Flow" pages as soon as you finish them. The purpose of this exercise is to look at your thoughts without judging or censoring. Right now, follow these instructions:

1. Find a quiet place where you won't be interrupted.
2. Use a journal if you want to keep these pages, or sheets of paper if you choose to shred them.
3. Get your watch or timer and prepare to write for five minutes. You can go longer if you want, but five minutes is a good start.
4. Write down whatever comes to mind. Since you have a lot of thoughts, you may abbreviate or just write down words. You can write down feelings and opinions as well.

5. Try not to censor or edit any challenging or difficult thoughts. If you find yourself editing, just allow yourself to write down those thoughts anyway.

Reflections on Writing and Riding the Flow

How do you feel about the contents of your mind? If you are judgmental of what you find, that's a normal reaction. My hope is that you can set aside the blame and shame for a moment and just look at the contents as you would an amazing and fascinating movie that is playing—starring you and your mind. If the movie is a sad one, you can just notice that it is sad. If the movie is a love story, you can just notice that it's a love story. What's important here is that you begin to pay attention to how the movie and the story line are always changing, always fluid.

At the same time, the movie is only a movie. You might be frightened by a particular movie but, when the lights come up, realize you are sitting in a theater and no longer identify with the characters and the plot. The same is true of the pages you just wrote on.

Get in the habit of practicing "Writing and Riding the Flow" two or three times a week to notice how the story or theme changes. See if, over time, you become less attached to any of the story lines as you turn up the lights on the movie.

Sensing the Body

If you pay attention just to your mind, you may be getting only half the story. Actually, mind and body are as intimately linked as two dancers performing the tango. The movement of one cannot help but affect the movement of the other. To really increase your AQ, or *attentional quotient*, you need to notice your body: its emotional tone, sensations, how it moves, and even its posture. This awareness is vital, because it can change how you relate to thoughts.

I still recall the time that I worked with Mary Lou, a thirty-year-old mother of three who was beset by fears about her children being harmed while engaging in normal activities, such as playing soccer or swimming. My work with Mary Lou began with my having her notice her fearful and anxious thoughts. Eventually, she progressed to noticing her body's reactions to daily events. Then one day she came to my office wearing a look of relief. She told me that, while driving her daughter to soccer practice, she noticed that her chest was tight and her breathing shallow, up in the higher part of her lungs. Although she didn't experience any anxious thoughts at this point (those usually came later, when watching her daughter play soccer), for the first time she became aware of a precursor to her anxiety. Instantly, she told herself to relax, and she started breathing more deeply—a skill that she had already learned and practiced. She discovered that she could use her body as an early signal or warning system.

Practice: Sensing the Body

For the next three minutes, practice sensing your body by following these steps:

1. Find a quiet place where you can sit uninterrupted.

2. Take several calming breaths and notice how the air connects you to your body. Your abdomen or chest may rise with each in-breath and fall with each out-breath.

3. Notice your feet on the floor and your body in the chair. Also, tune in to the position of your arms and hands.

4. Bring your attention to whatever may be occurring in any part of your body: the warmth in your hands, a tingling anywhere in the body, the feeling that comes from blinking, and the sensations around the eyes, mouth, and face.

5. Bring awareness, too, to your body's posture and any tension that may exist in your neck, your shoulders, or any other area.

6. Do not analyze feelings that arise. If your mind has a thought about a sensation, know that it is your mind, and let it go. Come back to the moment-by-moment sensing of your body.

Reflections on Sensing the Body

What was it like for you to experience your body close up? If your mind jumped in with thoughts or you found this difficult, that is a normal reaction. We live in a very "left-brained," thought-centered culture. By practicing tuning in to your body more throughout your day, you will bring greater clarity and focus to your whole being as you increase your AQ.

Identifying Emotions

The brain is profoundly wired to experience emotion. Instead of letting emotions overcome you, it's important that you learn how to identify them. Even if you are overwhelmed by emotions, research (Creswell et al. 2007) shows that you can actually be less prone to reacting to your emotions simply by naming them. Some basic emotions that have been found in facial expressions across cultures are anger, surprise, disgust, fear, sadness, and joy. Beyond these emotions are numerous secondary emotions like hurt, frustration, anxiety, love, guilt, shame, grief, optimism, boredom, serenity, trust, uncertainty, curiosity, and so on.

I've worked with many clients who were unaware of their emotions. The problem with this is that when you don't know your emotions, it's hard to understand the emotions of another person—and doing so is the foundation of empathy. Empathy builds trust, and trust builds strong bonds of understanding. You need empathy in order to develop romantic intimacy, closeness, and the ability to work through problems.

Practice: Creating a Feelings Journal

This practice is a good way to increase your emotional vocabulary, and you can learn this language, even if your family never taught this to you, by following these steps:

1. In your journal, draw three lines down a page so that you create four columns.

2. At the top of the far-left column, write "Event."

3. Label the middle-left column "Body Feeling."

4. Label the middle-right column "Emotion."

5. Finally, label the far-right column "Intensity."

As challenging life events or situations occur, write them down in the left column. Events here could include any difficult situation, whether at work or at home.

In the middle-left column, list all the feelings that occur in different parts of your body. In addition to noting where a feeling occurs—the chest or stomach or heart—also describe what it feels like. Is it hot, warm, tight, heavy, or hard?

Next, use the middle-right column as a place to give this feeling a name. Even if you have to guess at it, that's okay. Remember that for some emotions, such as anger, there can be other underlying emotions, including feelings of hurt or sadness. Even if your family of origin didn't possess any kind of emotional vocabulary, you can build your own by digging deep and observing your feelings.

After you have written down the name of the emotion, use the far-right column to rate the intensity level on a scale from 1 to 10, with 1 being extremely mild and 10 being extremely severe. Road rage, for example, would definitely be in the 7 to 10 range.

Reflections on Creating a Feelings Journal

Use your feelings journal often. Don't be afraid of getting to know your emotions and how your body expresses them. By doing this, you are becoming friendly with both your body and your mind. Eventually, you will gain a deeper understanding of how you respond in different situations. Best of all, the ability to name emotions actually helps you become more aware of them and improves your control over your feelings. Instead of just reacting to emotions, you will gain the skill to use the information as a means to fine-tune your joy compass.

Catching Fantasies

The mind is highly adept at wandering off into fantasy, which can be any flight of thought, imagined conversation, future-oriented idea, wish, or desire. According to research (Killingsworth and Gilbert 2010), people spend an average of 46.9 percent of their waking hours in fantasy, or mind wandering, rather than thinking about the activity in which they are engaged. What's more, the greater the mind wandering, the greater the unhappiness that people reported.

Have you ever stopped to think about how many fantasies you experience daily? What do they consist of? How long do you dwell on them? Do they appear at certain times of the day, such as when you are stressed, daydreaming, or avoiding an unpleasant task?

There is only one way to find the answer to these questions. You need to harness your attention to look at the nature and frequency of your fantasies.

Practice: Becoming a Fantasy Catcher

Choose a period during the day when you can devote time to catching fantasies, such as while driving your car or traveling somewhere. Turn off the radio and try to remove other distractions.

1. Look for themes that appear over and over.
2. When you get to a place where you can write down your fantasies, do so in a nonjudgmental way.

After a week or two of observing and writing down fantasies, you will have a better sense of your habits of mind.

Reflections on Becoming a Fantasy Catcher

Fantasy catching can be an eye-opening and worthwhile experience that brings full attention into your life. You are getting a glimpse behind the veil of how your mind operates and what it is attracted to or repelled by. Do you notice any repeating themes? Angry and confrontational themes may be stress inducing, while themes of traveling to exotic places may offer insight into a personal passion or a unique way to use your joy compass.

How Sublime

Don't give up on these practices for becoming friends with your mind and body. Give yourself credit for taking this giant step into self-knowing awareness. Approach this endeavor with a sense of lightness, openness, acceptance, and curiosity. You will likely discover more about your mind and body than you thought possible.

CHAPTER 2

Using Intention to Show Who's in Control

Unlike focused attention, which is the basic skill necessary for observing your internal and external worlds, intention is the steering wheel that helps turn your attention in the direction you want. Intention gives purpose to your awareness. It can give you the boost of energy and effort necessary to start and sustain any conscious choice—such as the intention to seek out joy and avoid negativity and unhealthy coping behaviors.

By mastering intention, you will gain greater confidence in your ability to turn away from anxiety-provoking TV news and angry blogs, as well as compulsive behaviors like impulsive shopping and emotional eating. With this greater control comes a feeling of fulfillment in knowing that you are making skillful, joyful, and beneficial decisions in your life.

Consider, for a moment, what life would be like without intention. Take a moment to reflect on examples from your own life or the lives of others. Without intention, you can be easily pulled this way and that by every little distraction, annoyance, desire, or craving, much like a boat that has no sail or rudder. Such a boat cannot help but be bounced around and carried along at the whim of each wave and the prevailing wind. Being skillful with your intention changes all of that. Meditation teacher and author Eknath Easwaran (2009, 200) wisely wrote, "The wind is always blowing, but we have to do the work of making our boat seaworthy."

Intention is a powerful tool for overcoming habits and even addictive behaviors that keep you from finding joy. With each intention, you literally transform your brain by wiring up new neuronal circuitry that sets a new course. Further, intention helps you sustain that desired direction.

The exercises in this chapter will give you the skills needed to align your joy compass so that you can safely navigate around any nasty weather conditions that you may face—even a hurricane looming ominously on the horizon.

Finding Balance with Intentional Breath

One of the best ways to calm down from stress and also to strengthen your intentional muscles is to blend breath with a mental intention. These two things are perfectly suited for one another. First, the breath turns on an ancient relaxation system that your body possesses. When you breathe in a specific way that will be described shortly, signals are immediately sent back to the brain's emotional core and negativity bias that, in essence, say, "Cool down. I know you're feeling anxious or upset or angry, but it's going to be okay. I'm going to help you think this through instead of just reacting." The body cannot ignore this message. It is literally wired to respond in a comforting and healthy way.

Intention then does its part by activating the area of the brain known as the prefrontal cortex, which is implicated in self-knowing awareness, empathy, impulse control, joyful attunement with others, and the ability to consciously bring the mind, body, and emotions into balance.

The Joy of Breath

If you have ever had difficulty breathing, due to asthma or any other condition, you can probably appreciate the joy of taking a nice, deep breath. I've experienced asthma myself on more than one occasion, and I remember how wonderful it felt to get my "normal" breathing restored. Because we breathe so often—taking about twenty thousand in-breaths and out-breaths in a single day—it's easy to take this gift for granted. Breath, as you will discover, is an ideal means of locating joy and peace in the moment.

The breathing style you will learn here is the same one you used when you took your precious first breath. This style has you breathing into the lower part of your lungs and is called *belly breathing* or *diaphragmatic breathing*. If you want confirmation that we are all born breathing this way, just notice any baby, and you will see how the belly—not the chest—moves up and down with each breath. Stress, however, can cause the breath to move higher into the lungs. When this happens, and it often becomes habitual in many adults, you are more vulnerable to stress—which results in the fight, flight, or freeze response.

The good news is that diaphragmatic breathing reverses the stress response. In about a minute, you will start getting the benefits of lower blood pressure, pulse rate, and respiration rate. You will cleanse the blood of the anxiety-producing chemical lactate, as well as release the feel-good neurotransmitter serotonin into the bloodstream.

In *Undoing Perpetual Stress: The Missing Connection between Depression, Anxiety, and 21st Century Illness*, Richard O'Connor (2005, 27) writes that continued high stress on brain and endocrine systems "eventually will lead to all kinds of bad outcomes—exhaustion, cardiac strain, kidney stress, muscle fatigue, damage to the digestive and circulatory systems." What would you be willing to pay to get a treatment from a doctor that would counteract this kind of stress-induced immune-system breakdown and damage? Well, the good news is that when you use the practice described here, it is absolutely free! I have worked with many clients who told me that learning how to breathe in this way was one of the most profound experiences of their lives.

To begin, you will want to know if your breath is high or low in the lungs. You can easily determine that by sitting in a chair and placing the palm of one hand on your chest and the other on your belly. Now, just breathe normally. Which hand do you notice moving? If you're not sure, look in the mirror as you do this, or have someone observe you. If the upper hand or both hands are moving, you are probably getting a shallow breath. This means that you are activating the body's alert and alarm system, and that you may be dealing with chronic stress. If the hand over the belly is the one that is moving, then you are turning on the relaxation system by practicing diaphragmatic, or belly, breathing. Everyone can benefit from learning how to belly breathe.

Practice: Belly Breathing

Use the following steps to experience the power of calming breath.

1. Sit up in a chair. Don't be rigid, but don't slump either.
2. Clasp your hands together behind your back. Just touching the hands is okay, as long as the arms are moved back. (This stretches muscles in the ribs and helps open the rib cage so that you can breathe more deeply.)
3. Let your abdominal muscles relax. (For women who have been taught to hold the stomach in, you can always do this in private if it makes you self-conscious.)
4. Breathe normally. If you feel light-headed or dizzy, you could be breathing too quickly or taking breaths that are much larger than normal.
5. Don't worry about whether you breathe through your mouth or nose. Just breathe naturally.
6. Exhale slowly to create a longer and more relaxing breath.
7. Place your attention on your abdomen. Don't force your stomach out. Simply notice how the abdomen naturally rises and falls with each breath.

8. If you want, use a visualization to help you imagine the breath, such as a wave rising with each in-breath and falling with each out-breath.

9. Continue doing this for one minute as you pay attention to getting the breath into your belly, and notice how your body feels.

Reflections on Belly Breathing

Did you notice that the belly area was moving more with your hands behind your back? What did your body feel like? Did it feel relaxed, calm, tingly, or warm? The important thing to remember is that you are changing your biochemistry by breathing in this way, as well as increasing the air in your lungs by ten times the normal amount. You can always experiment with an alternate arm position by raising your arms and clasping your hands behind your neck or head. This position also works by opening up your rib cage.

Practice: Daily Belly Breathing

The goal of this practice is to retrain your body to belly breathe on a consistent basis. Just as you learned how to breathe into your chest because of stress, you can relearn how to breathe for joy and peace. The following are a few tips to help you do this.

- Place colored stickers around the house—such as on the bathroom mirror, computer, TV, and so on—to remind you to notice your breath. Then, for one minute, place your hands behind your back (even when standing) and practice belly breathing.

- Place stickers where you will see them outside your home, such as on the rearview mirror of your car, your appointment book, and even the face of your wristwatch.
- Any time you feel stressed, anxious, upset, or angry, breathe diaphragmatically until you calm down.
- Belly breathe at night, when you are going to sleep or if you happen to wake up and can't fall back asleep.
- After belly breathing becomes natural, you can discontinue placing your hands behind your back or your head.

The Power of Intention

Intention is one of the most useful tools you can bring into your life. It is especially critical to wire up your brain's intentional circuitry, because it gives you the ability to veto any harmful action that you may be in the act of starting. Intention is like an instant short circuit that can block an offensive statement or behavior—and as a result, save you from having to make up for a lack of judgment or overwhelming emotions.

In *Mind Time: The Temporal Factor in Consciousness*, scientist Benjamin Libet (2004) described his work on the temporal nature of consciousness, which showed that when you prepare to take some kind of action or make a statement, you have about one-third of a second to decide *not* to follow through by using your intentional veto power. That may not seem like a long time, but the brain is very fast and can do several things even in just milliseconds. That is why one-third of a second gives your brain a whole lot of time to say no to an unkind statement or thoughtless action.

I remember when I worked with Ray, a man in his forties with a lifelong habit of making sarcastic remarks that harmed relationships and upset his wife. After working with intentional breathing for a couple of weeks, Ray came into my office and shared the story of how he had stopped midsentence while making a caustic remark during a dinner party. When his friends had asked why he had suddenly stopped talking, Ray had explained that he had intentionally vetoed a sarcastic thought—adding that he didn't want to hurt anyone's feelings. It turned out that his friends were curious, and after getting his wife's okay, Ray had shared his would-be caustic comment. "I was really proud of myself," he told me, beaming. "And they all laughed at what I stopped myself from saying."

Practice: Intentional Breathing

Breathing can easily be combined with intention. You will link a mental command to take a breath with the action of taking a breath. In this way you will also bring your mind and your body together in harmony. (To follow up on an earlier metaphor, you are training your puppy mind to follow your command.)

1. Before inhaling, state a simple and direct mental intention, or command, to breathe in. This can be any of the following phrases: *Create a breath, Inhale,* or *In-breath.*

2. After stating the command, follow up with the action of taking that in-breath.
3. Pay attention to the beginning, middle, and end of the breath. It's easy to give the command and then lose awareness of the full and complete breath. In this way, you are also observing the breath and using your attention.
4. Notice the pause between the in-breath and out-breath.
5. Before exhaling, state a simple and direct mental intention, or command, to breathe out. This can be any of the following phrases: *End a breath*, *Exhale*, or *Out-breath*.
6. After stating the command, follow up with the action of taking that out-breath.
7. Pay attention to the entire breath, including the beginning, middle, and end of the breath.
8. Continue doing this for one minute. Remember to belly breathe.

Reflections on Intentional Breathing

Did you find that it was easier to stay with the breath when you first set an intention? There are a lot of little things you can notice when you breathe with intention. When you take a long breath, you can be aware that you are taking a long breath. Likewise, when taking a short breath, you can be fully aware that you are taking a short breath. In addition, you can bring to each breath the joyful attitude that each breath gives you life, each breath gets you in touch with your body, and each breath soothes your body and calms it down.

Basically, the intentional practice you just used has three main elements:

1. Setting an intention to do something
2. Following up with an action
3. Paying attention to the complete action

In addition to observing how the body moves as you breathe, you can also observe any thoughts, emotions, or memories that arise. You can apply this three-step intentional process to anything you do, from brushing your teeth in the morning to doing chores or homework. Each time you apply it, you will be training the puppy mind to pay attention and be more disciplined and directed.

Your Intentional Life

You may not have given much thought to your existing intentions, even though they are shaping your life each moment. In order to create strong and purposeful intentions, you must first understand the unspoken intentions that are already at your side. For example, what do your present-moment activities and actions say about your current daily intentions relating to your job? Do they say that you are unfocused, irresponsible, unhappy, unmotivated, and miserable? Or, do they illustrate that you are focused, dependable, caring, assertive, eager, and hardworking?

What do your present intentions reveal about the relationships in your life? Are they centered on bringing support, love, and generosity to others? Do they keep you inspired to stay connected with significant others in your life? Or, do they show that you are self-absorbed, suspicious, mistrusting, jealous, anxious, and defensive?

What do your intentions say about how you seek out joy? Do your intentions promote security and health in your life, or are they risky and potentially harmful to you and others?

On a larger scale, what do your current intentions tell you about your life's purpose? Do they help you focus on longer-term goals? Are they congruent with your deeper values?

Practice: The Intentions Inventory

To take an inventory of your intentions, get four sheets of paper and label each at the top with one of these headings: "Job Intentions," "Relationship Intentions," "Daily Joy and Well-Being Intentions," and "Life Purpose Intentions."

1. Draw a line down the middle of each sheet.
2. At the top of the left column, write "Actions/Activities/Attitudes (Feelings)."
3. At the top of the right column, write "Beneficial/Harmful."
4. Starting with one of the sheets, write down the activities or actions that are present for that category. If you are listing job activities, make sure to state whether you are late or on time, what your attitude is, whether you like or dislike your job or your boss, and so on. Be totally honest about how you use your time and what your feelings are!

5. Opposite each left-column entry, use the right column to determine whether your intention is beneficial or harmful. You can just write "B" for beneficial or "H" for harmful.

6. Belly breathe as you go through this exercise. Do not judge yourself. Rather, think of this as an opportunity to bring new intentions to light.

Reflections on the Intentions Inventory

What did you learn about yourself by looking at your current behaviors and the intentions that are enfolded within them? Which ones would you like to change? Which ones would you like to change but are afraid you might not be able to? Let yourself sit for a little bit with the truth of your old behaviors and their intentions. What's important is that you have taken a step toward creating more helpful and encouraging intentions.

Right now, let yourself reflect on what it would be like to invite some new behaviors, activities, and feelings into your life. How would these things support the intention of greater well-being, closeness, and meaning in these four areas of your life? As you imagine this, notice how your body feels. Do you feel that your body is supportive of your desire to make these changes?

Practice: Statements of Intention

One of the best ways to ground yourself in a positive intention is to write it down. You can use the same four domains as previously used: family/relationships, work, life purpose, and daily joy. For each of these categories, write a single sentence that clearly states your intention. This master intention is like a mission statement that you can use to be sure that your actions, activities, and attitudes match up with your intention. The following are a few examples of *statements of intention*. I encourage you to set your own unique intentions—ones that express who you are and what you want from life.

- *My intention is to create loving relationships that manifest the values of respect, cooperation, kindness, generosity, harmony, and ease.*
- *My intention is to bring an attitude of deep appreciation and gratitude to my work and to always have my work serve others in a helpful and supportive way.*
- *My intention is to share the knowledge and expertise that I have gained in life with those who can benefit from it, bringing joy and meaning to others.*
- *My intention is to find daily joy in the little things that are already at my side and to share them with others, as well as be joyful for the happiness of others.*

Reflections on Statements of Intention

Feel free to keep revising your statements of intention. They can keep you focused. Read them often. Share them with someone you care about. You may want to keep your statements of intention tucked away on your computer or someplace where you can always connect with them. You can even laminate them and put them in your purse or wallet. The more you have a clear direction of where you are going, the easier it will be for you to locate joy. As you move into the next part of *The Joy Compass*, you will identify many new ways of integrating joy into each statement of intention that you have written.

Practice: Five Minutes of Moment-to-Moment Intention

This is an experience that can deepen your knowledge and your direct experience of intention. It will show you how complex even the slightest intentional movement or activity can be. It will also focus your mind and body on intention—so that other thoughts and sensations won't be as prominent or intrusive. Keep in mind that it is very normal for you to have a variety of thoughts, emotions, memories, and sensations intrude on your practice. Don't try to push them away. Simply notice them and return to setting your intention, following up with action, and observing the movement.

To begin, make sure you won't be interrupted for five minutes. It is best to do this in silence, at least at first. Eventually, it will be easier to interact with others while being intentional, but for now, try this alone or with someone else who is also doing the practice.

For the next five minutes, give yourself total permission to do whatever you want. You can stand up, get a bite to eat, walk around the room, make a cup of tea, or pet the cat. The only difference is that you will specifically set an intention before doing each action. There are really no limitations (other than answering the phone). If, for example, you are sitting and want to stand, you can set the intention to move forward in your chair. Feel how your torso leans forward and how your weight shifts over your feet. As you push up with your legs, know that you are pushing up. Devote yourself 100 percent to the experience of standing.

When you take a step, know that you are taking a step. Walking can be broken down into *Taking a step with the right leg* and *Taking a step with the left leg*. Feel the lifting of each foot, the movement of the foot as it glides through the air, and even how the foot touches the floor. Which muscles tense, and which ones relax? As you turn your body in a new direction, set an intention by stating, *Turning, turning*. Let the puppy mind know who's in control!

Should you choose to take a bite of food, be aware that you are entering an advanced area that is filled with many intentions. You might notice how your arm moves the food to your mouth, how the food changes from solid to liquid, how it tastes, and how many times you chew. You can set the intention to swallow, and wait to see how many minutes the flavor remains in your mouth after each bite. When your five minutes are up, intentionally return to your original place, and intentionally pick up this book, noticing the shape and weight of it in your hands.

Reflections on Five Minutes of Moment-to-Moment Intention

What did you find as you linked intention to action? Naturally, intention slowed you down. How present were you as you did each little thing? What was it like to go off "autopilot" and set the "robot" aside for a while? It's easy to walk robotically, but in doing so, it's easy to forget how much wonderful balance and how many gifts and abilities the body possesses.

Although in this practice, you used intentions for small movements, you can also be intentional without all the micro intentions. When walking, for example, you can just be aware of the larger intention "walking" as you place full awareness on the movements of your arms and legs. In this way you can move at a normal pace, with full intention and attention.

Refer back to this chapter as you continue your journey into joy, and may intention be with you every step of the way.

PART 2

Mindfulness Pathways to Joy & Positive Moods

CHAPTER 3

Laughter Really Is Powerful Medicine

Imagine for a moment that you are a cancer patient and your doctor prescribes a cutting-edge medication that can strengthen the immune system and significantly increase the body's natural killer, or NK, cells, which are an essential part of the body's defense system for fighting viruses and rejecting various types of cancerous tumors. Would you take the medicine? Or, suppose that you have high blood pressure or an abnormal heart rate and your doctor tells you about a proven therapy that takes just thirty minutes a day—and that can lower your blood pressure and reduce the risk of heart attack by a significant amount. In addition, you learn that neither of these therapies has any negative side effects. Would you be willing to begin the therapy?

The Effects of Laughter on Our Health

Such miracle medications and therapies really do exist. Yet you will not find them on any drugstore shelf or being created in a pharmaceutical laboratory. That is because they are, quite literally, the results of laughter, and research continues to provide positive results about how laughter affects our mood states and physical health. A study published in *Alternative Therapies in Health and Medicine* (Bennett et al. 2003) examined the effects that watching a humorous video had on cancer patients. While one group watched the humorous video, the control group of cancer patients watched a neutral tourism video. The results showed that stress decreased for those patients who watched the humorous video. Even more impressive was the difference in immune-system response, because the humor group showed a significant increase in NK cell activity. The researchers concluded (ibid.), "Laughter may reduce stress and improve NK cell activity. As low NK cell activity is linked to decreased disease resistance and increased morbidity in persons with cancer and HIV disease, laughter may be a useful cognitive-behavioral intervention."

Laughter is not just an intervention for physical illness. Laughter researcher Lee Berk (in APS 2006) studied how a hearty belly laugh primes your body for beta-endorphins to relieve depression, as well as produces human growth hormone (HGH) to help with long-term immunity. Humor not only positively transforms your body's stress system, but also helps you better cope with life difficulties when they arise.

Laughter actually scrubs out toxic chemicals and negative feelings, and it has been doing so for a very long time. New research indicates that laughter may actually have developed as far back as 12 to 16 million years ago—and not in humans. Marina Davila Ross and researchers at the University of Portsmouth (Davila Ross, Menzler, and Zimmermann 2008) found that primates possess the ability to experience empathy and possibly laughter. Groups of orangutans at four sites around the world were observed for facial mimicry of a gaping, open mouth: the equivalent of laughter. Human babies also automatically respond to smiles and laughter from others with an expression of facial laughter. This contagious, positive emotion of empathy and laughter among orangutan playmates likely has a survival value. The researchers explain (ibid.), "By mimicking emotional expressions of others, individuals are able to experience and understand the emotions of their social partners.... Until our discovery, there had been no evidence that animals had similar responses." Finding this social response in orangutans—which split off from the line of primates that produced humans—is like finding the missing link of laughter.

Laughter is an essential survival tool. Each laugh you take becomes part of your daily volitional awareness and attunement. It is a personal choice for the inner orientation of joy. That's why it's important to ask yourself the question: *What makes* me *laugh?* Let's find out.

Practice: A Personal Laughter Survey

When explorers Lewis and Clark went about surveying the Northwest, they took an extensive inventory of the plants, flowers, and animal life they encountered. They drew detailed pictures and also made maps of the new territories. In this practice, you are the explorer and surveyor of humor and pleasantness in your life and surroundings.

Take a sheet of paper with you each day for an entire week as you do your survey. Note where you find the most humor. As you do this, pay special attention to places, individuals, and situations. You can continue to add to your survey as you travel and visit new territories—such as sporting events, classrooms, lectures, shopping malls, grocery stores, and meetings. Make sure that no potentially humorous locale is safe from your prying surveyor's eye.

Your job is to do the following:

1. Locate all the local, exotic, and undiscovered humor and silliness in your territories and dwelling spaces at home, work, and so on. Are there certain individuals who make you laugh? Seek these persons out and keep notes on the level and duration of the humor you find. In addition, observe those things that possess humor potential and make note of them. They could be such things as funny signs, customs, and advertising. I once saw a sign in a store, for example, that made me laugh. It read: "Have you bought your beans today?" I don't know why, but it tickled my funny bone and got me looking for other oddly worded signs.

2. If you encounter a "Humoro sapiens," make a point of engaging it in laughter so that you can document its laughter ritual.

3. Note, too, what sights, sounds, textures, and so on have untapped humor potential. Write them down in your sur-

veyor's journal. This could be anything from advertising that makes you laugh to a humorous street sign to song lyrics that are plain silly or even nonsensical. Remember to cultivate a childlike curiosity about whatever you see. This is a mindfulness trait that lets you notice even everyday rituals, such as shaking hands or greeting others, in a fresh and lighthearted way.

The body is an excellent joy compass, so pay attention to your body and let it be your trusty guide to what is funny. If something brings a smile to your face or just makes you feel warm, bubbly, or good inside, then that's what counts.

Reflections on a Personal Laughter Survey

What did you discover about what makes you laugh? Did this survey help you identify new sources of humor in your life? Did you notice patterns in what tickles you? Does a wry turn of phrase, a pun, or another verbal joke put you in stitches? Is it visual humor that you really enjoy, or maybe a combination of verbal and visual? Perhaps more important, did you find that you smiled more this past week? Just anticipating humor can be a good thing. So keep looking for and finding new ways to laugh.

Lighten Up Those Serious Moments

While empathy and laughter may be contagious, our world is not in any imminent danger of a major laughter epidemic breaking out. On the other hand, the world's stress and negativity levels seem to be running wild. How is stress so potent that it threatens to steal our free will and turn us into robots that act out of anger and fear?

In the film *Falling Down* (Smith 1993), Michael Douglas plays the part of an alienated engineer who experiences a total stress meltdown. The engineer, whose vanity license plate reads, "D-FENS," goes off the deep end on a Los Angeles freeway on the hottest day of the year because he can't get to his daughter's birthday party. Being foiled in his attempt to accomplish a simple, decent, and good thing causes him to lose all sense of joy and hope. Actually, Douglas's character was overwhelmed by his body's ancient stress system and his knee-jerk reaction to stress. If he had known how to use his joy compass, he could have turned his predicament in a more positive direction. (Of course, that would have been a totally different and uplifting film.)

He could have done something amusing and absurd, like standing on top of his car to dance, preach, or tell jokes to his captive audience. He could have taken out golf clubs from the trunk of his car and gone to the grassy shoulder to practice his chip shots. Or, he could have picked flowers from the side of the road to create a traffic jam bouquet for other frustrated motorists and for his daughter. And, he could have just laughed for the fun of it, because when you are laughing, you are experiencing the heart of joy.

Laughter is a wonderful antidote to anger and other negative feelings. Whenever you feel stuck in anger, envy, jealousy, greed, blame, bitterness, cynicism, frustration, or unhappiness, your mind and body are awash in a biochemical soup that darkens your view of the world. That is the perfect time to laugh. As proof, ask yourself if you have ever been angry while laughing. Personally, I have had moments when my own anger was dramatically transformed by laughter. The moment I started laughing, the anger quickly dissipated, and it was difficult to imagine why I had been upset in the first place.

As a therapist, I routinely talk to clients about using laughter to improve their moods. I remember when Janice, a fifty-three-year-old woman, came to see me for depression and anxiety. "I haven't laughed in weeks," she commented during her first visit, noting that this was a sign that she was feeling blue. I asked about her favorite funny films and comedians, and she instantly named them. She followed instructions to watch funny films during the next week, which got her laughing again and feeling more like herself.

I'm suggesting not that laughter is a panacea but that it is essential for locating joy, which in turn gives us a sense of hope. Humor brings you back to a positive emotional state, which is necessary for joy to flourish.

Practice: Lightening Up

What do you take seriously? For example, paying the rent is a serious thing, right? Or is it? What are those things that push your "serious" button? Do critical comments from others push it? How about another driver who cuts you off? Maybe it's a sideways glance from a close relative or a disapproving frown from your boss? Then there are those things that each of us takes a bit too seriously about ourselves—like worrying what others are saying, thinking, or dreaming about us. Or, it could be the demands and expectations that you place on yourself regarding your desire to be perfect, successful, or respected. The point is that you may be conditioned to react to particular events in a knee-jerk fashion, whereas someone else can shrug off the same stimulus. By looking more deeply at your "serious" buttons, you can learn to respond in a lighter and more effective way.

1. Using a sheet of paper, write down those things that you spend too much time worrying about. Make a thorough list, including things big and small. I know someone in Portland who is angry at the rain. Considering how frequently it rains in Portland, it might make more sense to be angry at the sun!

2. After you complete your list, make an executive decision to laugh it off, let it go, and lighten things up. Yes, you heard that right—and you can decide to do that. Because if you don't, no one will!

3. If it helps, write down a "lighter view" for each of your "serious" items. The lighter view could be past evidence, for example, that nothing positive came from being too serious. You might even make note of others who don't worry, considering them as role models.

Reflections on Lightening Up

What is it like to see all of your "serious" items together on one page? Are there more of them than you imagined? Do you often strongly identify with your woes—even in a humorous way? The Yiddish word *oy* is used to express a personal exclamation of disbelief, dismay, sadness, and exasperation. Each time you decide to let go and lighten up for the day, you are letting go of the "oy compass" and choosing the joy compass.

Switch from "oy" to joy and see what a difference this makes in your sense of "in-joyment."

Practice: Joyful Breathing and Smiling

Each time you laugh, your breath deepens. But even if you aren't in a position to laugh hysterically—such as when you are interviewing for a promotion or taking your marriage vows—a good, deep, joyful breath is the next best thing. Diaphragmatic breathing, which you learned in chapter 2, is the first building block of humor, because it turns on the body's relaxation system and cools down the limbic system. But deep breathing is only the first part of priming yourself for laughter. Now is the time to transform your breath into a smile.

1. Again, let your breath flow naturally into your diaphragm. As you do this, let your entire face relax.

2. As you continue to breathe, imagine yourself as the *Mona Lisa*, with the corners of your mouth rising slightly. Imagine your eyes lighting up with happiness, and feel the area around your eyes glowing and raising slightly. Let your smile begin to grow, and as you do, feel a tingle of lightness and happiness in your cheeks. You may sense a tickle in your stomach, a feeling that is connected to your smile.

3. Now, let the full radiance of your smile shine outward. Let yourself relax like this, enjoying the feeling of contentment that comes from resting in a joyous smile—just smiling for the fun of it. There's no need to have a reason.

Even if your smile feels forced or artificial at first, allow yourself to smile fully and completely.

4. If it helps, imagine yourself in the presence of someone who always makes you laugh—even when you don't feel like it. Trust that your body will take over after you start smiling.

You can refresh yourself with a smile and a deep breath throughout the day. Smiling is universal; it's found in all cultures. Smiling is powerful because it changes your internal biology and feeling state. Smiling makes it easier to access pleasant memories, while frowning may trigger unhappy thoughts and memories. Think for a moment how you feel when you see another person smiling. Spread some smiles around today, and see if you don't notice a positive smile aimed in your direction.

You can even decide to wake up to a smile by placing a picture of a smiling person on your nightstand. Or, tape the smiling face onto your bathroom mirror so that it will be one of the first things you see in the morning. Don't underestimate how the smile and breath of hope can align your inner joy orientation. Keep them with you all the time. Smiling and breathing are two of the best techniques for relaxation and preparation for laughing that money can't buy. Throughout the day, ask yourself:

1. Where is my breath right now? Am I breathing shallowly, or am I getting the natural breath of joy?

2. Where is my smile right now? Am I frowning, or am I letting my smile enliven myself and others?

Reflections on Joyful Breathing and Smiling

How did you feel after letting yourself smile for no particular reason? Did you notice a change in your emotional state? Did you experience a sense of lightness or joy anywhere in your body? How could you practice smiling each day? Even if your smile is not reciprocated by another person, you can still experience positive feelings from each smile and joyful breath.

Laughter Memories

Have you ever thought of creating at least one powerful laughter memory each day for the rest of your life? Unlike that lifeless laugh track on TV, this is a real moment of inspired, out-loud laughter that is memorable and worthy of retelling—either to yourself or to others. A laughter memory can be any humorous event, thought, or observation that stimulates positive mood states that are joyful, uplifting, heartwarming, energizing, and euphoric.

Early this morning, for example, I tried to get my cat to laugh with me. To do this, I laughed out loud as I held him, and I also tried to tickle him. Nothing seemed to work, and instead of laughing, he looked at me with very wide and curious eyes, as if he didn't know me. More likely, he just wished he didn't know me. His odd expression made me laugh even more. I didn't succeed, but I am going to find a way to get him to laugh one of these days. Even if he's laughing at me, not with me, that will be good enough.

You can also find a laughter memory in one of your own foibles, idiosyncrasies, quirks, or embarrassing moments. I remember when I had a fountain pen in my pocket, only to have it leak all over my shirt during a counseling session. It was only when I stood up to say good-bye to my client that I felt the wetness of the ink. It must have been leaking the entire time, but the client had never said a word. After she left, I laughed at what she must have been thinking the whole time. I also cried (figuratively) at having to toss out one of my favorite Hawaiian shirts.

Sometimes, others are kind enough to share their laughter memories. One of my best friends, Randall, is a writer who starts his day at the local coffeehouse. He often buys a bagel and has developed a habit of tossing each fresh bagel into the air "to see if it is aerodynamic." He has performed this ritual hundreds of times, apparently never having had a mishap. Over lunch, he described how, on the morning of his birthday, he had flight-tested a fresh bagel by tossing it into the air. But instead of going straight up, this particular bagel—which was apparently highly aerodynamic—zipped out of his hand at a 90-degree angle (he swears he has no idea how this happened). The errant bagel flew over five feet away, zooming just in front of a woman who was reaching for her 20-ounce mocha adorned with a mound of whipped cream. The drone bagel got there first, blasting gobs of whipped cream and mocha all over the countertop and floor. As my friend described this story, I was in stitches.

Dismayed by the bagel incident, my friend decided to promptly go home and light a large red birthday prosperity candle that he had saved just for this day. He made another miscalculation and, while blowing out the candle, inadvertently sprayed hot red wax all over his white carpet. This second accident also had both of us laughing hysterically. Thankfully, he made the decision not to drive his car that day.

Practice: Creating Laughter Memories

Do you have any favorite laughter memories that come to mind? Whether you have many or just a few, let's look at how you can create more:

1. To begin, set the intention to create at least one special laughter memory a day. This will help you remain observant, alert, open, and more prone to see the humorous side of life.

2. Start a laughter memory journal to record your laughter memories. Write down your laughter memory at the end of the day or when the memory is fresh. Having these stories will help prime your laughter pump when you need a lift.

3. Here are several suggestions for locating laughter memories. Share funny articles or comic strips with others who like to laugh. You can also seek out "laughter yoga" clubs, where movement and laughter are combined to create daily, communal laughter memories. Another useful way to create a laughter memory is to simply recall a hilarious film or TV show. Make a list of your top-five funny films and watch them again. You can also combine a problem you are experiencing with laughter. By doing this, you are integrating two apparent opposites and creating an entirely new mind-body feeling state. Since no situation is completely bad, this laughter memory can help you

develop a broader and more humorous perspective on almost anything.

4. At the end of the week, look over your journal and review your laughter memories.

Reflections on Creating Laughter Memories

What do you think will be your biggest challenge to creating laughter memories? What will be the most exciting thing about doing this? Whom can you share your laughter memories with? By sharing your experiences, you are spreading joy, one guffaw and one smile at a time.

CHAPTER 4

Get an Attitude of Gratitude

What is the elixir that can turn unhappiness and discontent into emotional riches? It's gratitude, which stems from the ancient word *gratitudo*. It means to find what is pleasing or to give thanks. Gratitude promotes an attitude of appreciation, openness, kindness, altruism, and gratefulness, which can help you get unstuck from life's ruts. It points your joy compass toward a more spacious and enriching view of whatever may be happening in your life. With gratitude, you can find the gifts that were previously hidden from your sight. Gratitude shifts your perspective from what's missing in your life to what is present. It must have been gratitude that a wise person was referring to when advising, "Pray for what you already have in your life; that way your prayers will be instantly answered."

The Benefits of Gratitude

Gratitude is more than a warm and fuzzy feeling. Research shows that gratitude exerts a powerful effect on both mood and behavior. In four studies conducted on gratitude (McCullough, Emmons, and Tsang 2002), researchers found that feelings of gratitude correlated positively with a sense of well-being, optimism, and prosocial behaviors. (*Prosocial behaviors* can be thought of as positive ways of responding to others, including acting fairly, expressing appreciation, being willing to assist, being honest and ethical, and fulfilling your obligations.) Participants who practiced gratitude also expressed an enhanced sense of spirituality and religiousness. Interestingly, these studies found that gratitude was inversely correlated with negative mood states, such as envy, and such values as materialism. These studies seem to indicate that gratitude acts as an antidote for emotional stinginess and constriction. Whenever your compass points to true joy—as in the case of laughter, as discussed earlier—your attention is turned away from negative thoughts and moods.

Practice: Lifting Your Mood with Gratitude

Let's try an experiment right now to see the extent to which gratitude can shift your mood. Get a sheet of paper, and rate your mood in this moment on a scale from 1 to 10, with 1 being extremely negative, unhappy, or discontented, and 10 being extremely positive, happy, contented, or peaceful. Write that number on the top of the sheet.

Next, notice all the things that you appreciate or are grateful for. I'm not just referring to the big things that often come to mind—like health, shelter, a job, and so on—but also the myriad of little things that you can be thankful for. This could include how the sun feels when it warms your skin, the flavor of your breakfast cereal, and the fresh water that comes when you turn on a faucet. Don't be stingy when creating your list. Really, really look at all that's available for you on a daily basis! Let yourself soak in all that you have in your life. You may just need to look for what is present, even if it means looking in the refrigerator, in your closet, or in your office. Even if you feel that something is missing from your life, is there a way that it could actually be a blessing? Have you learned something from life's challenges?

Remember that gratitude can also include things you appreciate or find pleasant—like your favorite blouse or shirt, that keepsake or memento that you place on your desk, and so on. Write down all of these things on the sheet, and don't stop writing until you have at least ten items that meet the criteria for gratitude, gratefulness, appreciation, thankfulness, and pleasantness. After you get to ten, go for fifteen! How about twenty? Have fun as you do this. The point here is that if you are thankful for what is already in your life, then you will never be disappointed! When you have completed writing down all that you are grateful for, take some time to look this list over and let it sink in.

Now, it's time for you to rerate your mood level on the scale from 1 to 10. Write down this number and compare it to your original number.

Reflections on Lifting Your Mood with Gratitude

How much did your mood change? Did you feel a greater sense of contentment or peace when focusing on gratitude and appreciation? Are you surprised at what you may have been taking for granted? What is it like to know that you have so much to be thankful for? If you are still not able to tap into gratitude, reflect on people who are less fortunate than you, who have poorer health, or who have fewer resources and opportunities. Or, simply engage in a brief negative visualization of what your life would be like if you either lost what you have or didn't have as much. The purpose of this activity is not to feel good at another's misfortune or expense, but to see the truth of the goodness that exists in your life each day.

How can this gratitude practice help you revise your expectations of what you need to make yourself happy? Again, the purpose here isn't to make yourself happy with less, but to make yourself happy with *what is.* You can still have dreams and goals, but to make your happiness solely dependent on future expectations steals the joy from this precious moment.

Appreciate Your Strengths

One of the most crucial and fundamental forms of gratitude—although it often goes unnoticed—is appreciating your own strengths and good qualities. For example, do you find it easy to identify the strengths of others, but have difficulty locating your own? As a psychotherapist, I see a big part of my job as helping people identify and appreciate their own strengths. When people are under a lot of stress, they tend to forget their enduring personal strengths and resilience.

Many children's stories focus on locating and appreciating personal strengths. One cherished and timeless story, L. Frank Baum's (1900) *The Wonderful Wizard of Oz*, explores how fear and doubt—think of the evil witches and the confounding wizard—can make us forget and overlook our strengths. The scarecrow doesn't recognize his own intelligence despite displaying cleverness when needed; the cowardly lion repeatedly shows courage during his perilous journey; the tin man expresses enough emotion to prove that he already has a heart. By the end of the story, all of these characters appreciate and are grateful for their strengths that were there all the time—but had just gone unacknowledged.

We need to not only be thankful for our own strengths, but also take the step of reminding others of their strengths. Is there someone in your life—a child, parent, partner, friend, or colleague—whose strengths you appreciate and hold dear? When was the last time you expressed that information to this person? Helping others gain a deeper understanding of their values, strengths, and qualities is an important relationship-building practice. When I have couples share their partners' strengths with each other, the result is often very moving and poignant. Statements like "I didn't know you felt that way about me" and "It's been so long since you told me that" are common, as are expressions of delight, appreciation, and caring.

Practice: Locating the Hidden Strengths Within

If you had to name your personal strengths, what terms would you come up with? In *The Strengths Book: Be Confident, Be Successful, and Enjoy Better Relationships by Realising the Best of You*, authors Alex Linley, Janet Willars, and Robert Biswas-Diener (2010) identify sixty unique strengths that you can use to create a better life and improve relationships. They include such wide-ranging strengths as action, adventure, authenticity, compassion, connection, courage, detail, humility, innovation, listening, persistence, planning, self-awareness, service, and work ethic. In addition to those fifteen strengths, let's add an equal number that aren't in the book: being accepting, accessible, charismatic, collaborative, contemplative, energetic, faithful, generous, hospitable, loyal, passionate, playful, practical, questioning, and spiritual. Use this list of thirty strengths as a starting point. (I hope that gratitude or gratefulness makes your list!) Start now.

Locating Your Hidden Strengths, Part 1

This is a two-part practice. In part 1, you will name your own strengths.

1. Get a sheet of paper and write "My Strengths" at the top. Give yourself five minutes to write down as many of your strengths as you can name. As you make your list, keep in mind that this is not a time for humility (even if that is one of your strengths)! Remember that pride is also a strength. That's because it pushes you to strive for the

best, in addition to improving the quality of all that you do. Be generous and honest (another possible strength) as you consider what to include on your list.

2. Think about the strengths of friends, and see if you don't also possess these qualities.
3. When you think you have hit a wall and can't come up with any more strengths, set a goal of adding five new ones.

When you're done, give yourself an A+ just for trying this exercise.

Locating Your Hidden Strengths, Part 2

For part 2 of this practice, you will name the strengths of a significant person in your life. This could be a friend, relative, or partner. It could even be someone whom you don't especially appreciate or have an issue with! Your job will be to find the hidden strengths in this person. This could be more challenging if you choose someone who pushes your buttons, but you can still think of that person's negative qualities as strengths. Traits like stubbornness and denial, for instance, can be viewed as strengths because they can be used to overcome adversity—especially personal adversity, pain, suffering, and abuse.

1. On another sheet of paper, write the name of the person whose strengths you'll be identifying. Then, spend the next five minutes writing down these strengths.
2. To complete part 2, you will need to tell this person the strengths that you admire and appreciate in him. Know that as you do this, you are giving the gift of gratitude to another person.

Reflections on Locating the Hidden Strengths Within

What was it like to identify your strengths? Did you encounter resistance to taking on this practice? What was most surprising about doing this practice? Did you find yourself appreciating more good qualities than you had imagined? How can noticing and being thankful for your strengths give you a greater sense of confidence, peacefulness, and joyfulness? How does acknowledging your strengths affect your mood? Let yourself bask in the natural joy that comes from knowing your strengths.

What was it like to come up with a list of strengths for another person? Was it easier or harder than coming up with your personal strengths list? How do you feel about the idea of sharing this list with the recipient? When you do reveal these qualities to the other person, notice how it makes you feel, as well as how it affects the relationship. Last, consider using this practice regularly, as a way of sharing your positive feelings.

Compassionate Gratitude: An Engine for Helping Others

Gratitude is often defined as an inner feeling of thankfulness or gratefulness. But gratitude also has a real impact by producing compassionate action in daily life. A study in *Psychological Science* (Bartlett and DeSteno 2006) demonstrated that gratitude can actually elicit helping behavior, even when it comes at a cost to the helper—such as having the helper spend up to thirty extra minutes assisting another person. The idea that gratitude can generate compassionate behavior reveals its huge potential for making a difference in the world.

If you find that you have difficulty experiencing appreciation or gratitude in the moment, try recalling memories of when you felt these warm feelings. Can you recall a time when you received a helping hand from a neighbor, friend, or stranger? How did that make you feel? Do you remember if, in gratitude, you repaid that person at a future time? Maybe it made an impact on you, and you passed it on or paid it forward to someone else.

As chronicled in an article in *Parade* magazine (Wolf 2007, 5), Oprah Winfrey discovered the long-lasting power of compassionate gratitude at a very tender age. Sharing a story from her childhood, Oprah describes how her fourth-grade teacher "would tell me that I was just the smartest little girl she'd ever seen. I felt shiny in her eyes. It's why, whenever I see a little girl, I always stop to try to acknowledge her. I always try to have a shiny moment."

Oprah's story makes the point that those who are grateful are likely to help others. Personally, I can still vividly remember with deep gratitude the kindness and understanding given to me by my eighth-grade social studies teacher, Mr. Wilhelm, when I felt isolated and disoriented in a new school after moving from the city to the suburbs of Chicago. The gift of self-esteem that he gave me over forty years ago lives today as gratefulness and a desire to show similar compassion to others.

Compassionate action stimulates gratitude because it is self-affirming in every way, capable of transforming our suffering into joy. Gratitude in action gives us faith in the expansiveness and generosity of our spirit. Compassionate gratitude is shiny because it makes us feel alive and present. Most of all, compassionate gratitude is shiny because it gives us a memory and a story in which we are safe, trusted, and worthwhile. Just as Oprah's story of feeling shiny stayed with her a lifetime, you can build a storehouse of shiny memories through compassionate action for others. This is one of the building blocks of joy. Let's locate it right now.

Practice: Compassionate Gratitude in Action

To begin this practice, you will create a "Compassionate Actions of Others Inventory" that lists others' actions for which you are grateful. It might help to reflect on people in your life. Mothers—because they are generally nurturing—can be a good source for starting this inventory. How did your mother or parents show compassion? Did your parents' discipline help you learn how to apply yourself? Did it help you learn to be accountable? If so, add similar examples to your inventory. Did you have a wise and kind teacher who inspired you along the way? You might think about an encouraging word that you were given along the way and add that to the list. Also, reflect on those people who have acted as mentors in your life, taking care to make a note of their compassionate actions.

After completing the previous list, compile the ways that you can energize your gratitude by giving back. You can entitle this list "My Compassionate Gratitude in Action." Complete this list by considering all the ways that you could transmit your gratitude to others. If you are already spreading your gratitude, by either informally assisting others or volunteering, congratulations on making a difference. This is just an exploration—don't worry about doing everything on this list! The more you open up to the possibilities that are available, the more you can act compassionately in the moment.

Be as creative as you can when making this list. Don't censor any of your ideas. Who knows what possibilities may occur to you!

Reflections on Compassionate Gratitude in Action

How did you feel when you recorded those times when others helped you or showed compassion to you during a period of need? Did you recall old memories as you did this practice? Did your awareness of these moments stimulate a sensation of gratitude and thankfulness?

What was it like to compile the second list, "My Compassionate Gratitude in Action"? Did you find new ways of expressing your gratitude? How can you take a first step in this direction? Keep in mind that compassionate action can be something small. Mother Teresa, for example, performed a lot of small but caring actions over a lifetime—and that was what made her extraordinary. The actions she took were ordinary enough, but the devotion and persistence she applied day by day were truly monumental. As you share your compassionate gratitude, give whatever you are capable of giving. Know that even the tiniest action, when carried out from a place of gratitude, can be extremely significant and meaningful to the recipient.

Gratitude Is an Effective Coping Skill

Gratitude propels you toward joy because it effectively counterbalances stress, traumatic life events, and comparison with others. Thankfulness is a powerfully adaptive way to reframe or make sense out of almost any stressful or traumatic situation. Such was the case with Fred, a fifty-three-year-old man who came to my office after separating from his wife of twenty-eight years. Fred was disconsolate at the notion of getting divorced. He felt like a total failure and compared himself with his parents, who had been married for over fifty years. We focused our work on gratitude, and Fred soon grew to appreciate that he was lucky to move on from what was an unhealthy, controlling, and unloving relationship. Instead of comparing himself to his parents or anyone else, he gained a deeper understanding of what he really wanted in a partner. Even his feelings of loneliness were transformed into thankfulness for being independent and pursuing exciting, new activities.

Gratitude also helps us cope with unhealthy cultural attitudes and emotions born of greed, craving, materialism, and hedonism. Anyone can get hooked on the pleasurable feelings that come from getting that new car, relationship, or video game, although these feelings are temporary. The tendency is to fill the void of loss of pleasure with another "new" object and then another. Many people, for example, jump into a "rebound relationship" after a breakup or divorce. Unfortunately, relationships based solely on a craving for pleasure or avoidance of pain usually produce negative consequences.

Gratitude overcomes the need for short-term pleasure, because it helps you keep from taking what you have for granted. A sense of appreciation allows you to place your attention on all the positive things in your life. Most important, because you are less likely to be overly concerned about others' possessions or achievements, your joy will not be dependent on anything external. These are the benefits of using this powerful joy compass practice.

Practice: A Gratitude Journal

One way to get in the habit of noticing gratitude is to create a gratitude journal in which you can track things you are grateful for. You can write them down daily, or every third or fourth day. What matters is that you get in the habit of noticing appreciation and gratitude. Before long, you will have a personal gratitude library that you can look over any time you need an emotional jump start. Start your gratitude journal right now by jotting down three things that you are grateful for that happened in the past week.

In addition, each week take a few moments to think back on one person who has helped you or shown you kindness or caring during the week. Write down your feelings of thankfulness and appreciation for what it was like to be supported in this way. If you want, let that person know that you are grateful for her help.

Reflections on a Gratitude Journal

What was it like to reflect back on the past week in order to find gratitude? What do you think will be the most challenging aspect of this practice? What do you expect to be the most satisfying and fulfilling aspect? Do you anticipate becoming more attuned to noticing gratitude each day? Have you previously had the experience of expressing your gratefulness to another person? How do you feel about doing this more often? As you continue with your gratitude journal practices, your curiosity may lead you to ask others what they feel about gratitude. Listen to their stories and discover how this method of navigating to joy works in strange and beautiful ways.

CHAPTER 5

Finding Forgiveness

Who hasn't been abused, hurt, traumatized, or treated unfairly in some way? Whether you have been fired from a job, rejected in a relationship, or worse, you are a member of a very inclusive club. I don't know of anyone who has managed to avoid every form of mistreatment, rejection, and pain in life. Suffering at the hands of others or life circumstances is a universal human experience. It's what binds us together. It is also why we need forgiveness. Without forgiveness we remain locked in a jail cell of past hurt and pain, all the while missing out on one of life's greatest learning opportunities.

Consider that when you sit in that cell, you have labeled yourself as a victim and thrown away the key. Holding on to resentment, anger, and bitterness may provide some sense of vindication, justification, and solace, but it does not offer any hope of joy.

The first time I met Janice, a slender mother of a teenage daughter, I couldn't help but notice her tautly drawn skin and deep-set eyes. There was an undercurrent of tension and an almost imperceptible yet constant movement in her legs, even when sitting. She was very up-front about what she believed to be her problem. "I overexercise," she said, furrowing her brow. "It is badly affecting my health because I'm physically exhausted almost every day. Sometimes I even fall asleep at work." It was clear that her excessive exercise was connected to an eating-disorder problem. More important was the root cause of her unbalanced behaviors: severe verbal abuse by her parents and the need to control something in her life.

Janice's father was a strict disciplinarian who demanded perfection from his children. What's more, Janice suffered from having a hypercritical and abusive mother. "All the women in my family are highly critical, especially of their daughters," she said tearfully, adding, "I'm critical of my daughter, even though I don't want to be."

Janice was convinced that she didn't measure up to her parents' standards, so she pushed herself relentlessly at work and at home in order to make everything appear perfect. All that happened was that her health became compromised and every ounce of joy was sapped from her life. Ironically, Janice had become her own abuser. Janice tried several methods of changing her unhealthy eating and exercise patterns. There would be temporary improvements, but she seemed almost resistant to traditional therapy. Meditation and mindfulness helped somewhat, too, but it wasn't until she tapped into an ancient remedy for people who have suffered abuse or harm that Janice started being less hard, critical, and driven to perfection. That remedy? Forgiveness.

Forgiveness can take many forms. For Janice, it meant self-forgiveness through letting go of her own critical nature. She started with small things. First, she let her daughter pick her own time to start doing homework. Then, she started to let go of all the little behaviors that steal joy and time, such as meticulously arranging the order of cups and dishes in the kitchen cabinet each night after dinner. By finding forgiveness, Janice slowly began to accept and forgive her own frailties and imperfections, as well as her demanding inner critic.

Starting to Forgive

Whether others abuse us or we abuse ourselves, forgiveness offers a means of transforming suffering into joy. Consider that the 2,500-year-old Buddhist loving-kindness meditation traditionally begins with blessings of forgiveness: offering forgiveness to those who may have harmed us, asking for forgiveness from those whom we may have harmed, and, finally, forgiving ourselves for any harm we may have inflicted on ourselves. It is from the heart of forgiveness that we can take a small step toward inner love and joy.

Practice: Letting Go of the Inner Critic

In this practice, you will identify and befriend the inner critic that keeps you from embracing the joyful life you deserve. Sometimes the inner critic is hard to recognize, like the air you breathe but can't see. This practice will help you witness the critic.

1. Right now, draw a line down a sheet of paper. Label the left column "Inner Critic." Above the right column, write, "Letting Go."

2. In the left column, list those ways that the critic grabs your attention and keeps you locked up in a cell of pain and anger. The critic is expressed in many ways, such as perfectionist beliefs, overfocusing on past hurts, self-criticism, being right, mistrust, impatience, and anger.
3. On a scale from 1 to 10, rate how much this particular critic keeps you from finding joy.
4. In the right-hand column, write down how letting go will improve your ability to enjoy life—whether by giving you more time and more emotional freedom or by helping you grow past old hurts and frustrations.
5. Finally, write down one small, realistic, and achievable strategy for letting go of this critic.

Reflections on Letting Go of the Inner Critic

Did you uncover any criticisms that have been hiding in plain sight? In what ways does your critic affect your ability to seek deeper fulfillment or connection with others? Know that it will take time and practice to let go of old critical scripts or behaviors. Letting go is a first step. Remember to offer forgiveness to yourself when the critic reappears. Then, let go again. It takes time to rewire your brain for joy.

Forgiveness Is an Extraordinary Gift

The truth is that when you've been hurt, it's not so easy to forgive. Many people decide they simply cannot and will not

forgive the hurts they have endured. There are many reasons for this. First, they may feel that their anger and pain are completely justified, and often they are. In *Forgiveness Is a Choice: A Step-By-Step Process for Resolving Anger and Restoring Hope*, author and psychologist Robert Enright (2001, 47) writes, "When it is an immediate reaction to injustice, anger is normal and healthy, and no one should feel guilty about experiencing it. Anger is like alcohol: A little bit can be beneficial, but too much of it is a problem, even addictive."

No one is suggesting that you become nonchalant about the offense you have experienced. That would devalue you as a human who deserves love and kindness. But it may be worth asking yourself this question: *Is my anger keeping me from moving forward in my life? Is it adversely affecting my health? Is it holding me back from trusting and experiencing joy and love?*

Further, it's essential to understand that forgiving does not condone or excuse abuse. What was unjust and wrong will still be unjust and wrong. Neither does forgiving mean that you would want to forget the abuse, for to do so might mean that you could be harmed in the future. At the same time, you need to acknowledge whether you are obsessing over or clinging to the abuse memory so tightly that it obscures and erases the joy inherent in this moment. For these reasons, forgiveness is a choice—really, an extraordinary gift—that no one but you is capable of extending both to yourself and to the one who harmed you.

But first, it is vital that you consider the extent of your anger and whether you are ready to forgive. Forgiveness takes time. However long it takes, know that you are doing this for you. Whether the abuser or offender is alive, dead, or unaware of your forgiveness makes no difference. You likely have no control over that person or situation from the past anyway. What matters is that you can use forgiveness as a master key to open the cell that keeps you from touching joy. When you walk out of the cell, you are free, and the abuser has lost all power to keep you there. If what you have been doing isn't working, it's time to take this next step.

Practice: Exploring Anger

This is a journaling practice where you will reflect on and answer the following questions:

- *How long have I been holding on to my resentment or anger?*
- *How frequently do I think about the hurt that I have suffered?*
- *How frequently do I think about who caused my suffering?*
- *In what ways has my refusal to forgive affected other relationships in my life? How has it affected my health? My livelihood?*
- *How heavy a burden is this condition to carry around? If it were an actual weight, how heavy would it be? What color, shape, and texture would it be?*
- *What would it be like to live my life without this weight?*

Reflections on Exploring Anger

What stands out for you most after contemplating these questions? You have just taken the first step to examining the consequences of staying stuck in your story of being harmed, having endured injustice, or living with a history of abuse. Do you know others who have struggled with similar challenges? How did they move forward? History doesn't necessarily determine the future. You have the power to learn from it and to make new choices.

Transforming Anger and Physical Pain into Compassion

Forgiveness serves a psychological and spiritual need. It helps us heal emotions and gain a larger spiritual perspective. But can it also aid in physical healing? New research is examining the connection between forgiveness and various physical ailments, including hypertension, fatigue, and cardiovascular issues. Understanding this connection is vital because unrestrained feelings of resentment and anger make chronic pain treatment more difficult.

A study conducted by Duke University Medical Center's Pain Prevention and Treatment Research Program (Carson, Keefe, Goli, et al. 2005) examined the link between forgiveness and chronic back pain. Researchers studied sixty-one patients who suffered from persistent low-back pain. All the patients were assessed using several forgiveness measures. The study showed that higher levels of forgiveness were correlated with lower levels of reported pain and anger.

In a follow-up study (Carson, Keefe, Lynch, et al. 2005), researchers used a novel approach to working with anger and chronic pain. As a clinical intervention, they decided to use a loving-kindness meditation with a group of patients who'd had at least six months of chronic lower-back pain. The purpose was to see if this forgiveness-oriented practice would lessen pain, body tension, and anger.

Researchers used the loving-kindness meditation because it is a proactive means of focusing on affirmative thoughts and emotions. In the study, participants practiced the loving-kindness meditation in a small group for eight weekly sessions, each lasting ninety minutes. Then, subjects kept track of how much time they practiced the meditation at home. The results found that the intervention was successful in two important ways. First, those patients who practiced the loving-kindness meditation reported less pain and tension on the day of the practice, as well as reduced anger the following day. Second, the study found a negative correlation between the amount of time spent practicing loving-kindness each day and the level of anger. In other words, more practice produced even lower anger ratings the following day.

Whether or not you suffer from chronic pain, loving-kindness meditation points your joy compass in the direction of compassion and spaciousness. This practice opens us up like a blossom to the morning sun. Like sunlight, loving-kindness is a warm, affectionate, compassionate, and nondiscriminating love. It focuses on the well-being of all people, without regard to age, economic status, nationality, gender, or any other distinction. It strives to overcome fear and negative emotions that block feelings of trust, empathy, and openness. Whether your pain is emotional or physical, loving-kindness affirmations can help begin the process of transforming unhealthy and harmful emotions.

Practice: Loving-Kindness

Before you start this practice, here's an overview. As mentioned earlier, loving-kindness begins with a statement of forgiveness. Next, it warms us by sending feelings of safety, well-being, and love to us. Eventually, these warm feelings are sent out to other groups of people: teachers and family, friends, neutral people, unfriendly people, and, finally, all people.

State the following phrases mentally. As you do so, try picturing someone who cares about you and deeply wishes you to be well, safe, happy, and healthy. If you can't think of anyone, think of a memory where you experienced the unconditional love that you have for a child, a parent, a sibling, or even a pet. That is the kind of deep and abiding love that you will be sending to yourself—but without relying on the memory.

Find a quiet place where you can practice for up to five minutes to start. You can always increase the amount of time later if you want. Begin each session of loving-kindness with forgiveness by reciting these three statements:

- *May those whom I have either intentionally or unintentionally harmed forgive me.*
- *May I forgive those who have either intentionally or unintentionally harmed me.*
- *May I forgive myself for the times I have either intentionally or unintentionally harmed myself.*

Now, recite the following phrases over and over for the remaining time. You can imagine these statements as blessings or affirmations, or as coming from whatever source you want (spiritual, divine, and so on). Let yourself feel the warm glow as these caring and compassionate sentiments wash over you.

- *May I be happy.*
- *May I be healthy.*
- *May I be peaceful.*
- *May I be safe and secure.*

You may find that you want to add or alter a line or word so that the phrase more closely connects with you. Trust your intuition to find the right words—for example, *May I be loved, May I be appreciated, May I be forgiven, May I be blessed, May I forgive, May I be patient*, or *May I be joyful.*

If you wish, you may recite the following phrases to conclude your practice. These statements express your recognition of the universal nature of suffering and your desire to be part of the solution by opening to the transformative energy of compassion, love, and forgiveness.

- *May suffering ones be suffering free.*
- *May the fear-stricken fearless be.*
- *May grieving ones shed all grief.*
- *May all beings find relief.*

Reflections on Loving-Kindness

Do you feel lighter after practicing the loving-kindness affirmations? Does your body feel more at ease? Do you feel any less attached to anger or negativity? As you continue to work with this practice, notice the effects on your body and your mood state. Did you remember to recall a memory in which you felt deep love? Loving-kindness practice takes time. Eventually, you may experience the warm and enveloping feeling of safety and joy that it offers.

Don't be afraid to adapt or shorten the practice. If you aren't able to practice for several minutes daily, try the instant loving-kindness approach to transformation by stating the following phrases a single time, as needed, during the day: *May I be happy, healthy, peaceful, and safe. May others be happy, healthy, peaceful, and safe.* Personally, I use this abbreviated practice many times throughout the day when I want to get centered in joy, openness, and calm.

In particular, pay attention to those times when you feel constricted, tense, angry, and impatient. You might be waiting in a long line, frustrated on the job, or engaged in a misunderstanding with someone. At these times, you can counter negativity and locate joy by sending out these words of affirmation to yourself and others.

The Giving and Generosity in For-Giving

There is an obvious, but often overlooked, aspect of forgiving. At its core, forgiving is about being generous and altruistic, even when it hurts. Philosopher Jacob Needleman (2011), a contributor to the book *Beyond Forgiveness: Reflections on Atonement*, explores the cultural aspects of giving when he writes, "[T]he joy of selflessness...[is] there inside us, waiting, but the culture puts a crust around it for selfish reasons, telling us to *get, get, get*.... But it never tells you that what you have to get to is underneath the crust, which is your heart, longing not to get but to give."

Giving is embedded in all the wisdom traditions because it is an essential spiritual practice that is both uplifting and sustaining. One of the first ways of tapping into the enriching and empowering nature of giving is to reflect on all that we are given on a daily basis. Consider, for example, the air that we breathe; the food that we eat; the precious brain, body, and senses through which we navigate the world. Without such ordinary treasures, we would not be able to accomplish even the simplest of things. It's all too easy to ignore these natural gifts and focus on what we lack and want. The good news is that generosity instantly moves your joy compass in the right direction because it turns the tables on emotional and material stinginess.

Practice: Random Acts of Generosity

Imagine for a moment that you have the power to change another person's life. It is possible that each time you give generously to another, you reaffirm and circulate joy. Today, set a joy compass course for generously giving. However you decide to give, let yourself experience how it feels to share your energy, positive emotions, and kindness with others.

1. There are many types of random acts of kindness available to you. On a sheet of paper, create two columns. Write the heading "Emotional and Spiritual Generosity"

above one column and "Material Generosity" above the other.

2. Now, allow yourself to get creative and write down as many different forms that you can think of from each category.

   Random acts of emotional and spiritual generosity could be such things as offering a smile, giving a hug, letting someone go in front of you at the grocery check-out, using forbearance to refrain from criticizing someone, sending loving-kindness to people in need, sharing a compliment, being patient, offering the gift of listening, volunteering, and so on. Random acts of material generosity could include buying a coffee for the person behind you in the drive-through, giving away a favorite book or other item, and surprising someone with an unexpected gift or token of appreciation.

   Because these are random acts of generosity, open yourself to the possibility of giving when you don't expect it. Surprise even yourself! Where, how, when, and what can you give? Count the number of times daily that you perform these acts.

3. Finally, set out two small cups. If you want, label them for the type of generosity: "Emotional/Spiritual" and "Material." At the end of the day, put a penny in each cup for each time that you offered a random gift. This is both a gift to yourself and a reminder that you can add more pennies each day. These cups will also help you see which forms of giving you excel at—and which you can practice more.

Reflections on Random Acts of Generosity

How many different ideas for offering random acts of generosity did you discover? The secret is to set the intention to find joy through giving. You can also set the intention to give in new and exciting ways.

After you follow through on this practice, consider the following questions. How does it make you feel when you randomly give? Do you feel happier—more fulfilled and joyful? Do you find that this form of giving makes you want to give even more? Do you set expectations—such as getting a thank-you—from the recipients? What would it be like for you to give anonymously, without requiring anything in return? What form of giving (emotional/spiritual or material) do you find easiest? Can you think of a reason why the other type of giving is more challenging for you?

The practice of giving raises more questions than it answers. This is a very profound practice that provides new insights about yourself and others—which is another way that giving to others gives you something valuable in return. Keep in mind that your giving does not have to be perfect or meet some imagined standard to be valuable. Even the smallest random acts of giving, when from the heart, are huge monuments to locating joy right when you least expect it.

CHAPTER 6

Music Is the Magical Mood Manager

The sounds and beats of music have reverberated in the human soul and psyche for thousands of years, since perhaps even before the first bone was used as a whistle or the first slender branch was carved to form a flute. Ancient music specialist and researcher Iegor Reznikoff believes that early cave art of the Upper Paleolithic period (ten thousand to forty thousand years ago) was connected to singing or music.

A study by Reznikoff, published by the American Institute of Physics (2008), examined Paleolithic caves to test various sounds and pitches. The goal was to locate those places where vocal sounds, melodies, amplification, and acoustics were most ideal. Amazingly, almost 90 percent of cave paintings were located near ideal acoustic areas. According to Reznikoff, this provides evidence that ancient people celebrated art and music together in a ritualistic manner.

One thing is certain: Sounds exert the powerful influence of nature, from the drumbeat that mirrors the pulse of all life to the ancient flute that entices like the joyful and seductive revelry of a babbling brook. Musical instruments themselves signify the deepest expression of joy, peace, life passages, celebration, and war. Drums have historically been used to call on spirits during funeral processions, as well as send soldiers off to war and into battle; bells often have a religious or spiritual use by signaling time for prayer or repelling evil spirits; harps have traditionally represented angelic and sacred music, as well as magic and protection.

Perhaps most important is the new understanding that music is much more than a mechanical vibration that traverses the eardrum along the middle bones of the ear, down the auditory nerve, and into the auditory cortex. These vibrations are actually translated into electrical signals that reach the brain's emotional center and can cause the endocrine system to dance with hormones and neurotransmitters. This hormonal dance can dramatically shift the body's heart rate, respiration, immune-system response, and mood. In *The World in Six Songs*, musician and scientist Daniel Levitin writes (2008, 101), "[M]usic increases our alertness through modulation of norepinephrine and epinephrine…all the while bolstering our immune system through musical modulation of IgA, serotonin, melatonin, dopamine, adrenocorticotropic hormone (ACTH), and ß-endorphin (ß-EP)." These are hormones and neurotransmitters that uplift mood, increase feelings of pleasure, enhance mental flexibility, regulate the body's circadian sleep rhythm, and boost immunity.

Studies have even shown that recovery time after surgery can be reduced when soothing music is played during and after an operation. One such randomized and controlled study (Nilsson et al. 2001) examined ninety hysterectomy patients to see how exposure to music affected such things as pain, speed of recovery, and fatigue. Those patients exposed to music during and after surgery required fewer pain drugs, were more mobile in a shorter time, and were less fatigued than their nonmusical counterparts. In other words, the right kind of music has the ability to affect us at the very cellular level of our being.

Change Your Song, Change Your Mood

Of course, not all music is soothing. Music can prime you for almost any mood, from bliss, love, and pride to remorse, anger, and sadness. Even the language used to describe musical tastes, lyrics, and groups acknowledges the mood-altering power of music. There is, for example, an entire musical category named after moods—namely, easy listening "mood music"; The Moody Blues are an enduring icon of sixties rock music; and the popular thirties song "I'm in the Mood for Love" has been crooned across generations, from Nat King Cole and Frank Sinatra to Barbra Streisand and Rod Stewart, among others. In music, mood is king.

I remember the time that Mindy, a twenty-seven-year-old social worker, came to see me for extreme job burnout and stress-related anxiety. In order to understand what brought her joy, I asked her what hobbies or fun activities she typically engaged in. I often ask clients this question during the initial intake session. Without a moment's hesitation, she answered,

"Music. I love it because it just makes me feel good." I also discovered that Mindy's job involved lots of travel. She spent up to two hours a day, often longer, in her car. When I asked if she listened to music while driving, she frowned and said, "My car radio and CD player are broken. My husband and I are struggling financially, so I can't afford to buy a new one. There are other, more pressing things that we need to put first."

I recommended that Mindy listen to upbeat music when she arrived home after work and that she consider the possibility of moving a working car CD player and radio up in the budget hierarchy. Two weeks later, Mindy came into my office with a grin. "I can't believe it, but it worked!" she exclaimed as soon as she sat down on the pastel flower-patterned sofa in my office. Mindy's husband had agreed to alter their budget priorities and put music back in Mindy's car. No matter how drained she felt after a client session, Mindy was able to regenerate and shift back into joy by listening to and singing with the upbeat music of her liking. Music got Mindy squarely back on the road to joy.

Another client, thirty-five-year-old Karen, was seriously depressed after a recent relationship breakup and the fact that her roommate had just formed a new relationship. It was not that Karen wasn't happy for her roommate, but that seeing her roommate with a new boyfriend at the apartment reminded her of what was lacking in her own life. When I asked Karen if she listened to music at such times, she replied, "Yes, I go to my room and listen to music. It's the only way I can escape without leaving the apartment. But it doesn't help. I just get more and more sad and depressed." Then I inquired, "What kind of music are you listening to? Is it upbeat or sad?" Karen paused for a moment, her brown eyes looking upward as she reflected on my question. "Love songs," she said, "and come to think of it, they're all really sad songs." After hearing this response, I had Karen keep a log of the kind of music she listened to and whether it lifted or lowered her mood state. The logs provided solid evidence for her that she needed to listen to upbeat songs to counteract her sadness. Before long, Karen was consciously using her joy compass to locate upbeat music that lifted, not lowered, her mood.

Practice: Making a Mood Music Inventory

The music you listen to on a daily basis, or at various times of your life, can turn you either toward or away from joy. This practice will help you be more aware of how you tune in to music—and in turn, how music attunes you to different mood states. All you need to conduct your musical experiment is a sheet of paper, a writing instrument, and a watch or clock. Here's how you will conduct your personal experiment.

1. Create three columns on a sheet of paper. Label the left-most column "Mood Rating Before." Atop the middle column, write "Music Type." Last, label the right column "Mood Rating After." The idea here is that you will chronicle how you use music and the effect it has on you—and how long it takes until your joy compass starts working.

2. Begin by using a scale from 1 to 10 to rate your mood *before* you turn on music, with 1 indicating a low mood and 10 a joyful mood. Then, make a note of the time, or if you have a stopwatch, start it.

3. Next, experiment by choosing to listen to a particular type of music. There are optimistic songs like George Harrison's "Here Comes the Sun" (which I listened to earlier today to help me brighten up, despite the persistently cloudy weather outside my window); upbeat songs like Bobby McFerrin's perennially popular "Don't Worry, Be Happy"; lamenting tunes like Elvis Presley's "Separate Ways" and Patsy Cline's "I Fall to Pieces"; and uplifting spiritual songs of forgiveness, such as "Ave Maria" and "Amazing Grace." You can also find songs in other categories, such as those that are sentimental, nostalgic, and historical. The goal is to find music that turns your compass toward joy—although you may also discover what music turns you away from joy.

4. Music does not need lyrics for it to move your mood in a positive direction, so try experimenting with instrumental music, from classical to blues to techno to jazz. Let yourself sing along, and feel free to adapt the lyrics. And if your body tells you to clap your hands, snap your fingers, tap your feet, swivel your head and shoulders, wave your arms, or dance like a dervish, follow its lead.

5. When you have finished listening to one or more songs of a particular type of music, notice your mood state and write your rating in the right-hand column. Also, write down how much time has passed since you started this experiment.

You have just identified what music helps you locate joy and how long it takes for you to get your neurochemistry happily dancing.

Reflections on Making a Mood Music Inventory

How long did it take for your mood to shift to a more positive place? How dramatic was the shift? If you initially rated your mood as 3 and it went up to 6, for example, then you doubled your joy. To think that you can do this in a matter of minutes is to harness the empowering energy of music. At what times during the day would you benefit from using music to locate joy? What life events would necessitate using your joy compass in this way?

Get creative in thinking about how to use this mood elevator. If you are recovering from an injury or illness, you can enlist music to speed up the healing process. If you are recovering from a divorce or the loss of a loved one, find music that soothes and supports. If you are experiencing feelings of anger, locate music that enhances feelings of calm, compassion, wisdom, spaciousness, and understanding. Keep using this practice to identify and locate joy when you need it.

Singing for Relief from Stress and Depression

Do you like to sing? Do you sing in the car? Do you perform songs of your favorite artists in the shower? You don't have to have perfect pitch to enjoy the benefits of letting your lungs fill deeply with air. For years a friend of mine, who is now in his eighties, has been known to croon in any willing venue. His operatic voice has brought joy to audiences at churches, restaurants, weddings, farmers markets, and sporting events. He frequently and spontaneously breaks into song while dining—quite a surprise to patrons and restaurant owners alike. One restaurant got such favorable reviews that they decided to make his appearances a weekly featured menu item!

In addition, it doesn't even matter if you are tone deaf; you can still activate joy with music. A fascinating doctoral dissertation and research study (Sandgren 2005) found that amateurs who received singing lessons actually experienced greater feelings of elation and joy than did experienced opera singers. According to the study, it is the act of self-expression and self-actualization in music that creates joy and reduces stress. Worrying about things like achievement and outcome can interfere with getting a true reading on your joy compass.

This study affirms the point that music is effective for finding joy right now, in this precious moment. Yes, there can be joy in achievement, but that joy is conditional and short-lived. For this reason, the secret to keeping your joy compass pointing to joy is to get immersed in the moment.

Practice: Singing Just for the Fun of It

By singing just for the fun of it, you'll get the healthy benefits of lower blood pressure and reduced stress that come with taking a diaphragmatic breath as you sing. Singers and performers understand the value of getting the air into the deepest part of the lungs. This lets singers extend notes and control pitch as they exhale.

1. If you are still practicing your belly breathing from chapter 2, you may want to take three or four belly breaths as a

warm-up for this practice. While singing, pay attention to taking a full breath.

2. Now, choose a song that makes you feel good. You may want to draw on a song that is connected to a positive memory from childhood, high school, a family gathering, or some other memorable event. One of my favorite songs is "Take Me Out to the Ball Game," which I love to sing in a crowd while rooting for my Chicago Cubs. Singing this song helps the entire crowd find communal joy and the hope that their team will win.

3. Whether your song is traditionally communal or personal, belt it out with a light heart and a smile. This is especially useful in the car, when someone rudely cuts you off. Even if you are shy, you can do this alone, where no one is listening. If you're not shy, try singing for others at karaoke or wherever you can. Another option is to hum tunes, a favorite practice of Thomas Jefferson, who was known to hum old Scottish tunes or hymns at his home in Monticello.

4. To complete this practice, create a playlist of songs that you can sing for different occasions. You can build several focused playlists, such as songs for a stressful workday and songs for transitioning from home to work and from work to home. How about a playlist for the weekend, a vacation, or a romantic date? You can even create a chores playlist for when you are washing the dishes, doing laundry, or mowing the lawn.

Reflections on Singing Just for the Fun of It

How did you like singing for no particular reason? Did you get your breath into the lower part of the lungs? Did your song tap into a favorite or memorable time from your life? What playlists did you create? How can you make sure that you will use your playlists?

You may decide to create a literal playlist that you can use on mobile devices. This way, even if you are in a location where you can't sing, you can still enjoy listening to playlists for various occasions when joy is called for.

From Sound Pollution to Nurturing Sounds

You probably can identify the music and sounds that you like, but what about the unwanted ones? Every day, urban and suburban living features a barrage of artificial sounds, including buzzing leaf blowers, beeping car alarms and traffic signals, rumbling freeway traffic, unmuffled exhaust, and the grinding gears of garbage truck hydraulics. This doesn't even include the myriad of sounds that we are accustomed to hearing at home: the hum of appliances, noisy toys, video-game explosions, and blaring TV commercials.

Noise pollution and congestion can result in a mental state that is equivalent to having a room filled floor to ceiling with disorganized clutter. Humans are extremely sensitive to sound, and sound congestion can be a major stress inducer that disturbs your ability to get calm and centered. In an article published in *Southern Medical Journal* (Goines and Hagler 2007), research was examined concerning the growing and adverse effects of noise pollution. According to this survey of the field, noise affects several vital life areas, causing sleep disturbance due to environmental noise, hearing impairment, cardiovascular issues related to increased stress, impaired task performance, increased social agitation, and annoyance. Noise pollution was also found to contribute to health issues like anxiety, nausea, headache, and reduced sense of well-being. What's more, children are particularly vulnerable to the effects of unwanted sounds.

I once worked with Ralph, an easily agitated man who worked in customer service in a very noisy manufacturing environment. He revealed to me that when he was younger, he enjoyed fishing and going out on the river. Hearing this, I suggested that Ralph incorporate a visit to the river into his commute to work each morning. He would use the time to get calm as he listened to the sounds of nature and reflected on how water flowed and never got stuck. The next week, Ralph came in to see me, looking much more relaxed. "I am the water," he said. I must have looked a little surprised by his proclamation, because he instantly clarified, "What I mean is that I can feel the flow. I can be like the water. Instead of responding with anger, I can let myself flow and be cool like the water. Water finds a way around and through anything. Even if a volcano spews into the water, it doesn't harm the water, because water transforms into steam." For Ralph, the sounds and images of water acted as a metaphor that pointed his compass needle squarely at joy while countering negativity and noise pollution.

Practice: Identifying Nurturing Sounds

Take a moment to think about the last several times you really let yourself tune in to the music of your natural surroundings.

1. Write these experiences down on a sheet of paper. Perhaps you recall the sound of crickets at nighttime, the rhythmic sound of the ocean, the gentle pitter-patter of raindrops, the wind rustling through the treetops, and the sounds of your favorite animal or pet. If you have a particularly fond memory of a sound, write that down as well.

2. Now that you have identified nurturing sounds, you need to find ways of locating them. Identify how you may hear or recreate each sound you wrote down. If you aren't near water, for example, you can still obtain a similar soothing effect by setting up a small fountain on your desk or playing a CD that features the sounds of water. Nature music abounds, from forest music to water music that you can use to lull yourself to sleep.

3. You can do the final step of this practice when you get the chance to visit a nearby natural space, whether in your own backyard, the courtyard where you work, or a nearby park. When you get there, pay attention to natural sounds that may be present, such as every chirping bird, croak of a frog, and gust of wind. In a mindfulness class that I taught, I had students go outside and listen intently to all the sounds of nature. It had recently rained, and one student was surprised to discover that she could actually hear the soft sucking sound as water absorbed back into the earth.

Reflections on Identifying Nurturing Sounds

What did you discover as you identified nurturing sounds? Was there a pleasant sound from your past that you recalled? Were you able to find a way to bring soothing sound into your life? Remember that this could also mean eliminating harsh sounds, whether on TV or elsewhere. How easy or difficult will it be for you to bring nurturing sounds into your life?

Last, make a commitment to seek out the sounds of nature weekly or whenever you need calming. Even if nature seems silent, let yourself intently tune in to the quiet music of the trees, the silent hymn of the blue sky, and the rhythms of the living earth. Rest in harmony with this natural music as far from noise pollution as you can. Pack up your smartphone and stow the electronic gear. You may be surprised at the peace the resulting sounds of silence invite.

CHAPTER 7

Contemplation and Meditation

As you read and reflect on *The Joy Compass*, you are steeping yourself in the ancient tradition of contemplation. The word "contemplation" derives from the Latin *contemplum*, meaning to set aside time and space for observation and interpretation. The practice of contemplation spans thousands of years of human history and, like all things, has evolved. In the more expansive terms of the twenty-first century, contemplation can be defined as exploring and experiencing deeper levels of being, awareness, self-knowing, and meaning—both individually and as shared with others. Contemplation is how we create our reality through meaning and ideas, as well as gain shared insight with others along the way.

The Different Types of Contemplation

As a means of setting your joy compass, contemplation is expressed in a rainbow of shapes and forms: sound and chanting, dance and movement, reading, mindfulness, meditation, dialogue, and prayer, to name a few. The nearly four-thousand-year-old Hindu scriptures of the *Rig-Veda* contain the earliest known hymns and mantras that were used in a contemplative way. In the sixth century, Gregorian chant music revolutionized the music of the day. Ritualized dance—such as that of Sufi dervishes in the twelfth century—mesmerizes us with its grace and dignity. Stylized forms of reading, such as divine reading, or *lectio divina* from the ancient Christian tradition, let us touch the essence of words and meaning in a fresh and exciting way. Mindfulness and meditation are contemplative practices for bringing attention, focus, and willing acceptance to each unfolding moment. Prayer is yet another contemplative practice intended to make space for a greater sense of peace, purpose, understanding, and joy. All of these contemplative practices have at their core the human need to participate in the world with others, to gain meaning and purpose, to have a voice and to be heard, and to love and to be loved.

Practice: Your Contemplation Style

What form of contemplation best suits you? This practice will help you determine how to find a method that works well with your learning style.

1. Using a sheet of paper, create two columns. Label one column "Hobbies and Pleasurable Activities" and the other "Personal Learning Style."

2. Now, proceed to make a list of all the hobbies and activities you enjoy. This may include looking at sunsets, taking a walk, enjoying a hot bath, bike riding, doing crosswords, writing in a journal, reading, singing or listening to music, talking with others, taking time for solitude, gardening, playing sports, doing yoga, going to parties, and so on. In particular, include those hobbies or pleasurable activities that you have historically done, even if you are not engaging in them at this time. In addition, include those activities that you have *thought* about trying but haven't yet. The reason for identifying those things you already like is to find a style of contemplation that can work for you, not to force you into something that you might likely lose interest in.

3. After you have completed your list, you will identify your unique learning style or strength, which we will then correlate to one or more contemplative practices. These strengths fall into seven categories: language, sight, hearing, movement, natural world, relationships, and personal insight/spirituality.

4. You can decode your hobbies and activities by looking at the following examples. Then, determine the correct category for each. Notice, too, that many activities fit into multiple categories.

   Your strength is *language* oriented if you like such things as reading, writing, keeping a journal, crosswords, word games, puns, word jokes, speaking, and telling or listening to stories.

Your style is *sight* oriented if you enjoy activities like visiting museums and art fairs, looking at sunsets, photography, painting, doodling, quilting, knitting, astronomy, motorcycling, bird-watching, watching and playing sports, visual games, and appreciating colors and fashion.

Your strength is *hearing* based if you are sensitive to sound and enjoy listening to music, going to concerts, dancing, singing, humming, or playing an instrument; or if you like to hear ocean waves and chirping birds.

Your style is *movement* oriented when you engage in swimming, walking, yoga, stretching, hot baths, jogging, hiking, biking, quilting, knitting, painting, sculpting, competitive sports, and less competitive sports like horseshoes, shuffleboard, and Frisbee.

Your style is *natural world* focused if you enjoy hiking, hunting, fishing, boating, the beach, camping out, archaeology, learning about natural shapes and objects, finding your way around new locations, sitting in the park, and farmers markets.

Your abilities are *relationship* oriented when you typically enjoy friends, a committed relationship, volunteering, book clubs, social clubs, church activities, planning or going to parties, empathizing, teaching others, and public spaces and events.

Your strength is *personal insight/spirituality* directed when you get pleasure from learning about yourself, praying, meditating, reading and reflecting, thinking about your purpose, going to lectures, engaging in spirituality, being in solitude, and seeking out silence, nature, and wisdom.

5. Now that you've identified your strengths, let's convert them to contemplative practices that may work for you.

   Language contemplation: Centering prayer, mantras, chanting, affirmations, spiritual study groups, classes, and expressing gratitude.

   Sight contemplation: Meditation on an object, gazing at the sky, mindful walking meditation.

   Hearing contemplation: Chants; mantras; group singing; hymns; playing and sharing spiritual, religious, and meaningful music; affirmations; mindfulness of sound.

   Movement contemplation: Yoga in its various forms, tai chi, qigong, breathing practice, ecstatic dancing, mindful walking, and labyrinth walking.

   Natural world contemplation: Sky-gazing meditation, centering with nature, mindful walking or hiking, gratitude, and mindful gardening.

   Relationship contemplation: Religious and spiritual groups, shared nonjudgmental dialogue with others, prayer, chanting, philosophy groups, mindfulness, and sharing contemplative practices with others.

   Personal insight/spirituality contemplation: Meditation, mindfulness, reading, prayer, chants, mantras, affirmations, gratitude, and solitude with nature.

Reflections on Your Contemplation Style

Which contemplative practices fit best with your personal style? Which have you tried in the past? Which new ones would you like to try? How could you take the first step to learning a new contemplative practice? Which of these contemplative practices could be the basis of a regularly structured contemplative practice?

Contemplating with Meditation

In addition to the calming belly breathing practice that you learned in chapter 2, there is an ancient meditation practice that focuses attention on the mind itself. Called *insight meditation*, its goal is to see the mind and things clearly as they are, without embellishment. It is done simply through labeling your thoughts. Okay, it's not so simple, because it takes practice. The good news is that there are many benefits to be gained from using insight meditation to find the joy setting on your compass. For one, you won't be subject to the whims of your mind's many distortions and fantasies, which can lead to unhappy emotions.

One of a series of ongoing studies about the practice of mental labeling (Lieberman et al. 2007) used functional magnetic resonance imaging (fMRI) to see how the labeling of emotions affected various brain regions. In the study, participants were exposed to photographs of people's faces displaying upset emotional expressions, such as angry or fearful. Viewing faces like these normally increases activity in the brain's emotional center and produces a biochemical stress response. But the study showed that when people labeled the emotion they saw in each expression, the brain's internal stress circuit was inhibited. Instead, other areas of the brain, in the prefrontal cortex, got activated. It is that part of the brain that strengthens mindful awareness and helps us process emotions rather than react to them. This may also be why talk therapy, or putting words to feelings, helps people feel better.

In the case of insight meditation, you regulate the brain's negativity by watching it intently, in a nonjudgmental and neutral way. By noticing such mental events as anxiety, fear, sadness, and so on, you clearly witness the mind's ongoing movie of opinions, interpretations, and judgments. These additional layers are like filters or sunglasses that color and distort how you view things—especially if these filters are arousing the stress response.

This meditation practice can help anyone who is experiencing reactivity. It was even used effectively with prison inmates in India during the early 1990s. Over one thousand inmates at Tihar Prisons in Delhi (Khurana and Dhar 2000) practiced insight meditation, and subsequent analyses demonstrated an overall positive effect on behaviors and attitudes, especially in reducing feelings of anger and vengefulness. Other courses (see, for example, Meijer 1999) designed to help inmates detoxify habitual negative states of mind have been conducted in the United States with similar success.

Practice: Insight Meditation

Insight meditation is a method of approaching mental thoughts and bodily sensations that arise by giving each thought and sensation a label. In this way, you shine the light of your awareness on the workings of the mind. This way of labeling thoughts acts like a tollgate keeper that tracks everything that passes through the mind.

Find a quiet place to sit, in a chair or on a cushion. Sit in an upright, dignified position and breathe diaphragmatically throughout this meditation. To begin, you will practice for five minutes. That's enough time to get a taste of this meditation, and you can extend the duration the more you practice it. You will close your eyes during this meditation. Read through all of these instructions before you begin your practice.

1. Begin creating a comfortable flow of breath until you get a nice rhythm. Imagine that you are keeping about 10 percent of your awareness on your breath. Notice the fullness of breath, the in-breath, the pause between breaths, and the out-breath. If you want, you can even label your breathing by silently repeating *In* and *Out,* or *Breathing in* and *Breathing out.*

2. Your mind will inevitably wander. When it does, you can repeat silently, *Mind wandering, mind wandering,* and then refocus your attention on the breath.

3. Since your eyes are closed, the image of someone or something might appear in your mind's eye. If this happens, just let the tollgate keeper track it by saying, *Seeing, seeing, seeing,* until the visualization disappears. Similarly, if you happen to hear something, the tollgate keeper can keep track by labeling that as well, by stating, *Listening, listening, listening.*

4. The tollgate keeper will track everything in this way. Should memories arise, just make a note of this by stating to yourself, *Memory, memory, memory.*

5. During moments when the mind is quiet, return to your breath, again mentally stating, *Breathing in* and *Breathing out.*

6. Whatever arises in your mind's eye, such as anxiety over a future conversation, planning for tomorrow, resisting the practice, or just thinking, you can use whichever phrases are accurate to label what you are noticing.

7. Even if you become aware of the need to swallow, label it, *Intention to swallow, intention to swallow.* You can do the same thing if you need to move your position. Just set your intention and then move, saying, *Moving, moving, moving.*

8. It is natural for the body to grab your attention as you sit. If you notice a physical irritation of any kind, simply label it, such as *Pain, pain, pain,* or *Itching sensation, itching sensation, itching sensation.* Do your best not to immediately scratch the itch or remove the pain, but notice it and see if the sensation goes away. It usually will. Noticing pain without fighting or resisting it can be useful. Place your awareness on it and see how pain is dynamic. This is also a lesson in dealing with and breaking through pain in everyday life—be it emotional or physical.

9. As you practice insight meditation, you will gain a deeper understanding and appreciation of the mind. You may start to notice that thoughts are not necessarily facts.

> They are temporary and don't persist for very long. You can gain a deeper understanding of the body's sensations too. Just watch the show with curiosity and see what you find.

You can also use this method to be mindful of any activity in which you are engaged. When you eat, you can silently state, *Eating, eating, eating*. When you are sitting down, you can stay present by thinking, *Sitting, sitting, sitting*. Any time your mind wanders off, you can bring it back to the body and the sensations you are experiencing in the moment.

Reflections on Insight Meditation

What was it like for you to notice your thoughts and label them? What kinds of things interfered with labeling your thoughts? Were there noises, sensations, or memories that drew your mind elsewhere? Did you remember to label the interferences? What about the emotions and feelings you had about sitting like this for five minutes? Whatever your experience—boredom, anger, frustration, or bliss—you can label it in a neutral way, like a tollgate keeper who counts the cars passing through.

What did you learn about yourself or the nature of your thoughts by spending five minutes focusing in this way? If you have never done this kind of meditation before, you may have noticed that your mind seemed more active. That's a normal response for someone who is watching the mind in this detailed way for the first time. You never knew how active your mind could be. This is a gentle means of making friends with your mind, your thoughts, and your sensations.

Decide how long and how frequently you want to devote time to this practice. You may be surprised at how quickly you start to feel the benefits of greater peace and calm with your thoughts.

Contemplating Nature

It seems that our brains are wired for nature's healing touch. Its ability to regenerate and renew us is part of our myth and lore. Now, research in the field of *attention restoration theory*, or ART, is helping us understand that nature can actually restore focus and attention. The field began in the 1980s, almost by happenstance, when Stephen Kaplan and colleagues at the University of Michigan (quoted in Jaffe 2010) recognized how, during finals and other intense periods, students seemed to prefer peering out the window at nature over engaging in other activities. His curiosity piqued, Kaplan began studying the connection between nature and attention.

According to ART, we have at our disposal two distinct styles of attention. The one that we use when focusing on a task, solving problems, or making decisions is called *voluntary attention*. This is the purposeful and highly directed form of attention required of students, nurses, businesspeople, electricians, teachers, lawyers, therapists, bank tellers, teachers, and others who need to pay close attention to tasks. Voluntary attention is thought to deplete the brain of energy. In my work as a therapist, for example, I have encountered several high-school students who complained of being mentally exhausted and fatigued after a day of problem solving and learning at school—only to face hours more of homework in the evening.

Then there is the second style of attention, the one that has to do with nature. This is called *involuntary attention:* a highly engaged form of attention that lets the mind rest. Research shows that nature is highly attractive to involuntary participation. One study (Kahn et al. 2008) that makes this case put ninety office workers under stress. The workers were divided into three groups of thirty. One group worked in an office with a blank wall and no windows. The second group worked in an office with an HDTV plasma screen that displayed a real-time image of nature. The third group worked in an office with a glass window facing out onto a natural scene. The results showed a significant improvement in heart-rate recovery after stress in the group with the real window, compared to those workers who faced a blank wall. The workers in the room with the HDTV plasma display fared no better on heart-rate recovery than the group with the blank wall.

An overview of how nature does more than simply provide cognitive benefits was published in the *Association for Psychological Science Observer* (Jaffe 2010). Observation of natural landscapes can reduce symptoms of aggression, anger, and depression. It seems that nature, even in small doses, lets you use the joy compass to find peace and serenity.

The exploration of attention also raises some interesting questions. How does television, for example, affect attention? Is TV a positive method of escape from depleted attention? The goal of television is to capture your attention and maintain your focus, not to let you engage with it in a free way, such as by changing the channel or shutting off the set. If you watch a program that turns on the stress response or upsets you, then you will likely stay glued to the set—while worrying at the same time. To use attention as you deem fit is to access your joy compass.

Practice: Centering with Nature

This is a short and simple practice that takes only a couple of minutes. I have worked with students, teachers, businesspeople, and others who have used it as a way to get refreshed quickly.

If you are able to get outside and experience this practice with a large tree, that would be ideal. But you can also do this practice with any indoor plant.

1. Go outside and stand near a particular tree. Choose one that looks interesting to you. You may like the color of the bark, the shape of the trunk, or the way the branches and leaves reach skyward. Before starting, place your hand on the tree. Let yourself feel the stability of this living organism. Trees are the largest living things on earth—both extending far beneath the ground and reaching high above it. Let yourself rest for a moment in appreciation of all trees—which help maintain our world's delicate ecosystem.

2. Next, let go of the tree and step back to where you can see the entire tree, from the very top to the bottom. Let your own feet and legs stabilize and balance you as solidly as that tree.

3. Start at either the bottom or the top of the tree, and slowly let your gaze wander along the entire tree. As

you do this, notice all the little details in the coloration of leaves or needles, and notice the texture and shape of the branches and trunk. Absorb everything you can from this—nature's gift.

4. When you have finished, gently move your focus to another natural sight—a tree or flower, the broad and spacious horizon—as you let go of any tension.

Reflections on Centering with Nature

After you have experienced this practice, ask yourself how it affected your mood. Did your ability to return to a task seem improved? How long did it take for you to get centered? By bringing a touch of nature into your home or workspace, you may get the benefits of this practice on a daily basis.

CHAPTER 8

Mobilize Resources through Affirmation

Affirmations have the power to move and inspire. The right affirmation can give you the positive energy to move forward when you feel stuck, gloomy, sluggish, or negative. Affirmations also make a powerful collective and communal impact. Whatever your political persuasion, take a moment to recall recent presidential campaign slogans. Which ones lifted your spirits? Which felt hollow or self-centered?

Why use affirmations? To some people, affirmations may seem disingenuous, a form of brainwashing, or simply a massive ego massage. The power of an affirmation, though, comes by genuinely opening yourself to the positive energy that stimulates optimism, energy, and enthusiasm. Ultimately, affirmations are about being available to the possibility of greater joy.

Dealing with "Shoulds"

When I met with Eric, a thirty-year-old man with an impressive history of overcoming drug use, I learned that he had been clean and sober for over three years. He came to my office because of social anxiety and low self-esteem. Eric was constantly filling his mind with negativity and self-blaming thoughts like *I can't go out to meet people because I'm overweight and don't look as good as other people*, *I don't have anything worthwhile to say*, and *I'll just end up embarrassing my kids and wife*.

When I first broached the idea of using affirmations, Eric bristled. "Why should I make up a bunch of stuff about myself that isn't true?" he asked. "Well, you have a choice," I responded. "You can keep telling yourself you hate yourself in so many words, or you can start loving yourself. Isn't it better to open the door to the possibilities in your life?" From the very first time that Eric started using mindfulness to become more aware of his self-blaming and self-rejecting thoughts and view himself in a more neutral way, he was shocked by what he learned about the contents of his mind. I still remember the day in my office when, after learning a technique to help him notice his self-blaming and self-critical thoughts, Eric burst into laughter and said, "If I heard those same words coming out of someone else's mouth, I'd think it was ridiculous!"

One of the first exercises that I used with Eric was to have him catch his use of the word "should." Often, "should" carries with it feelings of guilt, shame, and self-blame. The word "should" is often code for *I'm not really measuring up*, *I can't be happy unless I achieve _______________*, *Things are supposed to be different from how they are*, *I can't accept myself as is*, and *I* *must be perfect and can't make mistakes.* If you experience these kinds of thoughts or beliefs, it may be worth asking yourself, *Whose little instruction book of "should" am I really following?* Who *said I should?* Why *should* I?

This is not to say that you can't have your own standards and goals, but to say that turning them into a set of rigid and demanding expectations for yourself or others is a killjoy. After just a week of practice tracking his "shoulds," Eric returned with a newfound sense of awareness and spaciousness. Instead of being trapped in his "shouldness," he was beginning the supportive process of transforming negativity into affirmation.

Practice: Catching the "Shoulds"

Did you ever hear the following phrase, which is a paraphrase of something psychologist Albert Ellis was frequently known to say? Don't "should" all over yourself. (It sounds a lot funnier if you say it out loud.) But it's actually a very serious idea. This practice is a mindfulness method for getting to know your "shoulds" so that they don't beat up on you and turn your joy compass toward a negative setting.

For this practice you will start a one-week "Should Journal" to chronicle your "should" usage. For each day of the week, try to catch as many "shoulds" as possible. Write down each entire "should" statement that you catch. If you find that you are getting upset with yourself—*I shouldn't be saying "should" so much*—congratulate yourself because you have just caught another "should"! Take a neutral attitude as you ferret out these self-critical commands that you have been automatically heeding. In fact, you get an A+ just for paying attention to the "shoulds."

Reflections on Catching the "Shoulds"

What was it like as you paid attention to your "should" statements? Did you find more or less of them than you thought you would? Were there themes around your "should" usage? What was the context for the "should" statements? Were they used in relation to work, relationship demands, chores, or beliefs about others' behavior? How does it feel when you say "should"? What's the intensity of your voice?

Fortunately, the next exercise will provide a replacement word that will move you in a more positive and effective direction. As you create your journal, you can use the following practice as a way to transition out of "should" thinking and into a less judgmental and opinionated view of things.

Practice: Replacing "Shoulds" with "Coulds"

This is a very simple practice. Go back over your "Should Journal" and cross out the word "should" in each of the statements you wrote down. Next, replace it with the word "could." You now have a "Could Journal."

When you think about it, "could" is a liberating word because it's all about choice. Yes, you *could* try harder at work, school, and so on; you *could* be a better partner or parent; your child *could* help with the chores or do homework each night.

Read aloud the new "could" statements that are in your journal. Naturally, you don't have to wait for a week to use "could" as a substitute for "should." Make a point of switching from "should" to "could" the very instant that you notice each "should" statement. Start today and enjoy the freedom and joy of "could."

Reflections on Replacing "Shoulds" with "Coulds"

How do the "coulds" make you feel? Do you experience more lightness? Are you more relaxed or at ease? Do you feel more open and accepting? By using "could," you are setting your joy compass toward self-kindness by sculpting your language in a more gentle and forgiving tone. Use of the word "could" can open your mind to new ways to achieve your goal. It can lead you to explore your feelings about a particular situation, rather than leave you stuck in a negative and harsh point of view that doesn't accomplish much other than to deflate you or others.

The Language of Affirmation

The everyday language we use helps us navigate through life. Language is the narrative road map through which we gain meaning, and it can encompass how we approach and feel about almost anything. While physical and sexual abuse of children has been the subject of many studies, researchers only recently began focusing on verbal abuse. One study (Teicher et al. 2006) explored the effects of verbal abuse by parents and the risk factors that it produces. The researchers concluded that verbal abuse was a potent type of maltreatment that produced changes in the brain's emotional core: the limbic system. Verbally abused children in the study displayed greater anger, aggression, depression, and problems relating to other children. If verbal abuse from others is this harmful, it's not much of a stretch to imagine how we can cause self-harm and create self-limiting beliefs through inner verbal abuse.

Since most of us understand what constitutes abusive language, it's important to understand what makes a good affirmation. Affirmations can take a variety of forms. They can consist of full sentences or individual words, or even take the form of a mantra. They can be recited out loud, sung, or stated internally, as well as shared with others. This diversity is much like the diversity in music, which is constantly evolving. The ability to evolve our language—and our affirmations—is a testament to the flexibility of the human brain. In *Healing the Mind through the Power of Story: The Promise of Narrative Psychiatry*, psychiatrist and narrative therapist Lewis Mehl-Madrona writes (2010, 158), "We humans are under much less genetic control than any other species. That control has shifted to include social control of behavior.... We don't have an innate language without social learning." Mehl-Madrona makes the point that our brain structures are shaped by listening to and learning from others.

No one is predestined to repeat a family history or pattern. Even if you have the same genes as other family members, how you interact with the environment actually turns genes on and off. This means that you are not the sum total of your genes. No matter how critical others in your family may have been, you don't have to repeat the same tired script or walk in the same footsteps. Access your joy compass by infusing your personal life narrative with affirmation, as well as paying attention to how others craft affirmation.

Practice: Transforming Old Scripts into New Affirmations

Sometimes, our old scripts get so entrenched and become so much a part of the brain's wiring that they simply run automatically. Noticing these old programs is the first step to rewriting them as more optimistic and affirmative scripts. For this four-step practice, you will use a situation in which you struggle. Here are some possible general areas from which to choose:

- Social anxiety
- Finding friends and developing a social network
- Speaking and participating in groups
- Finding success in a chosen field
- Overcoming loss or grief

Or, you may have a more pressing and specific situation you face, such as:

I can't say no to taking on extra responsibilities at work.

I am afraid to ask for a raise.

I get impatient with others and can't stop myself from getting angry.

Using a sheet of paper, create three columns. From left to right, label the three columns "The Situation," "The Old Script," and "The New Affirmation." After you have done this, take these four steps:

1. To begin, write your chosen situation in the left column. It may also be helpful to write down the joy-sapping emotions that accompany that situation, such as sadness, frustration, fear, anxiety, impatience, worry, doubt, anger, disappointment, guilt, shame, embarrassment, and others. All of these emotions that match the old script are causing your brain's emotional core to send stress hormones throughout the body and brain.

2. In "The Old Script" column, write down all of the old scripts or programs. As an example, let's find a few old scripts from one of the previous situations: *I deserve a raise at work but am afraid to ask for one.* Possible scripts for this situation are:

   I fear that they'll turn me down.

   I worry that I'll be fired or demoted.

   I should be able to do all the work they give me.

   I'm too old to start over. I won't be able to find a job anywhere else.

   As you write down your old scripts, it's important to recognize how they directly affect how you feel and behave. They are a powerful narrative that you are seeking to change. Don't be afraid to dig deep and write them all down.

3. Using "The New Affirmation" column, challenge each limiting script with a more spacious perspective. While there may be some truth for you in the middle column, there is also truth in finding a more positive, broader view of things. This affirmative perspective can include evidence that challenges the old script, such as *I know other people who have found new jobs. In fact, there is evidence that people have many different careers in a lifetime.*

   You can derive evidence from your own life, from people you know, or even from historical figures. Mark Twain, for example, went bankrupt at the age of seventy, at which time he went on a world tour and rebuilt his fortune. Rather than believe he was too old to work, Twain must have had an affirmative inner script that helped him move forward.

   An affirmative script can also include an action plan, such as *I will make a list of all the reasons why I deserve a raise.* Make sure that your affirmation is written as an "I" statement. And because joy is located in the present moment, you also want your affirmation to reflect that. For that reason, consciously use the present tense when you construct your affirmation. So, instead of writing, "I will be a success in a new job," phrase your affirmation in such a way that it opens you to the positive possibility inherent in your situation. Such a statement might look like this: "I am a proven hardworking person who has a lot to offer the right employer," or "I can find a job where people appreciate and respect my efforts and skills."

   Finding affirmative statements can be a challenge if your old scripts are very strong. Don't give up. There is always a new affirmation waiting, even when the old script seems to be written in stone. Remember to use all three elements, including an action plan, evidence, and a present-tense possibility statement to counter the negative scripts.

4. Once you've written the new affirmations, it's time to rehearse. You need to practice the new affirmations until they become natural for you to say. You will need to know them well in order to counter old scripts when they arise. The better you learn the new affirmations, the better they will work on your behalf. It can help to practice saying them while looking in the mirror, paying attention to your expression and emotions as you rehearse.

Reflections on Transforming Old Scripts into New Affirmations

What was it like for you to put your old scripts on paper where you could see them? Can you better understand why the old scripts affected your behavior? Sometimes, seeing old scripts written down can make them seem less real and powerful.

How easy or challenging was it for you to create the new affirmations? Have patience with yourself as you go through the process of locating these new possibilities. It is also worthwhile to notice how you feel as you recite the new scripts out loud. Do you feel more confident, at ease, positive, or assured? That difference alone can make creating the new affirmations worth the effort. As you feel different, you can start to behave in a more optimistic and hopeful way.

Using Focused Affirmations

Every affirmation comes wrapped in a focused intention. You can use an affirmation for the purpose of finding greater confidence, tapping into self-love and fulfillment, overcoming loss and grief, revitalizing health, improving mood, embracing forgiveness, and deepening spiritual growth.

A study conducted at the University of Kentucky College of Nursing (Peden et al. 2001) examined the effect of focused affirmations and other cognitive techniques on college women with depression. The women were randomly placed in one of two groups: a no-treatment group and a cognitive-intervention group in which affirmation and thought stopping were taught. An eighteen-month follow-up found that the women who had learned affirmation showed a significant decrease in negative thinking and symptoms of depression, compared to the no-treatment group. The affirmation group also showed a greater increase in self-esteem.

The Sanskrit word *mantra* often represents the practice of repeating a word or phrase in order to focus the mind. While such a practice does sharpen attention, it can help us think about almost anything in an affirming way: from the loss of a loved one and letting go of old hurts to feeling healthier and more energetic. Let's try a practice designed to help you use the power of a simple word or phrase.

Practice: Using a Word as an Affirmation

Look over the following list of words. These words are just a starting point, and I encourage you to add to this list on a separate sheet of paper if you think other words or phrases might appeal to you. In addition to mantras used by religious traditions, you can consider using popular phrases that also contain wisdom, including "This, too, shall pass," "It's only a temporary setback," and "Tomorrow is a new day."

Your goal is not to choose a word, but to let it choose you. After reading slowly through the words, notice whether any of them speaks to you concerning what you may need right now. Each time you look through the list, narrow down your choices. Finally, find a single word to which you feel a strong connection. Don't analyze this too much. Just go with your feeling.

You can also tweak these words by turning them into a short phrase, such as "May I be loved," "I am calm and peaceful," or "I am open to acceptance."

Acceptance	Forgiveness	Nature	Safe
Appreciative	Fulfillment	Now	Security
Calm	Happiness	One	Spacious
Comfort	Harmony	Optimistic	Suffering free
Craving free	Health	Pain free	Tolerance
Earth	Joy	Patience	Trust
Empowerment	Laughter	Peaceful	Understanding
Energized	Lightness	Prayer	Unity
Flexibility	Listening	Resourceful	Water
Flow	Love	Restful	Well-being

Once you have found a word or phrase, use it to center your mind. Find a quiet place, either at home or in nature, where you can close your eyes and repeat the word mentally. To start, do this for five minutes.

A few guidelines are worth mentioning. Repeat your word or phrase in an effortless way. Don't force it. Let it come naturally, like the breath. If your mind goes elsewhere—and it will—just gently notice that you have stopped saying the word. Then, start repeating it again at an easy, comfortable pace. You do not need to synchronize the word with your breathing. Just settle in with it.

You may feel a positive or negative sensation arise in your body or mind. If this occurs, your mind will be drawn to that sensation. If it is negative, you don't have to push it away; if it is positive, you don't have to cling to it. Usually, these sensations will dissolve, and you can return to your chosen word. If you feel too uncomfortable at any time, just open your eyes and let yourself continue another time. You are always in control when you do this practice.

Reflections on Using a Word as an Affirmation

What did you notice most about repeating your word or phrase for five minutes? Did you feel calmer? Did your mind get more focused? Just because you chose a particular word doesn't mean that you must stay with it. Give yourself permission to experiment with other words or phrases.

How can you develop a daily mantra or affirmation practice? It might help to set a time each day to practice for a few minutes. You can even remind yourself that your affirmation is keeping your joy compass needle turned toward new possibilities. With your compass set, you will be less distracted and better able to locate joy.

CHAPTER 9

Get Grounded in the Here and Now

Advertisers devote millions of dollars to helping us find what will make us happy—as if we were unable to figure that out for ourselves. Consumers save up to buy items or activities that promise satisfaction. But what is it that really delivers the goods on locating joy? Is happiness the *activity* in which you are engaged? Is it getting that new, improved *thing* that you just plunked down money on?

The Benefits of Being Present

A unique study conducted by psychologists at Harvard University (Killingsworth and Gilbert 2010) used a web-based program (trackyourhappiness.org) to randomly contact subjects via their phones. When contacted, each subject noted the activity in which he was engaged and whether his mind was attending to that activity or wandering elsewhere. Last, the subject rated his level of happiness.

The study found that people were least happy when they were resting, working, or using a home computer: times when their minds were frequently lost in daydreaming. They were most happy when grounded in the body and the present moment, which included such activities as making love, exercising, or engaging in conversation. Researcher Matthew Killingsworth (quoted in Bradt 2010) points out, "This study shows that our mental lives are pervaded, to a remarkable degree, by the nonpresent. Mind wandering is an excellent predictor of people's happiness. In fact, how often our minds leave the present and where they tend to go is a better predictor of our happiness than the activities in which we are engaged." This confirms what mindfulness masters have long known: that it's not the activity in which you are engaged that makes you happy and joyful. Rather, it is how present you are with that activity.

Your presence determines your happiness. How simple; how sublime.

Practice: Surfing the Breath

In chapter 2, you practiced intentional breathing. Because breath is probably one of the best ways to get grounded in the body, we're going to use this practice again, but with a twist. You will integrate visualization with each breath as a way to keep you focused on this breathing moment.

Each breath is a marvelous thing. It builds like a wave, rising ever higher to reach a peak. Then, like an ocean wave, it pauses, unable to maintain this shape. That's when it curls over with natural grace, breaking and crashing with a sense of relief. Finally, the breath subsides, and just like that wave, it merges into the shoreline, disappearing quietly into the sand. This calm lasts only for a moment of pause, until the next wave arises to a crescendo. With the breath, you are constantly living in a symphony of waves, with no two exactly alike.

With this practice, you will imagine the breath not just filling your lungs and pushing on your abdomen, but also as a wave that fills and moves throughout your entire body. If you want, picture an actual wave rising as you feel the breath increasing and building.

To breathe in this way is to sense and surf the whole body with each breath. Like a surfer, you need to stay in touch with the wave from its beginning to its end. Rather than allowing you to take the breath for granted, surfing the breath gets you balanced and centered and alive.

As you surf the breath, make sure you don't lose contact with it. As you exhale and the wave of your breath subsides, notice how the body responds. Is there a moment of calm and repose throughout the body in the pause before the next wave starts to build? Does your heartbeat slow for even a beat or two? Do you feel a release of tension in your hands? Can you let go of tightness and tension as you surf the subsiding wave toward the shoreline?

Start surfing the breath anytime during the day. See how being present in this way brings peace and joy into your body and life.

Reflections on Surfing the Breath

Did you ever think a breath could be exciting? Did you find joy in surfing the breath? Did you contact your body in this precious moment? Where was your mind while you were surfing the breath? Was your joy compass pointing in the negative or positive direction? When you get proficient at surfing the breath, your mind won't be elsewhere. That's why surfers love to surf the ocean! It brings them fully into the present moment. If they are elsewhere, they will take a tumble.

How will you surf the breath during your day? How can this practice help you? Can you use it while sitting at the computer? While you are at work? How can you surf the breath as a means of bringing yourself back to the present-moment activity in which you are engaged?

Don't forget that you can surf the breath at night when you are trying to go to sleep. This is an especially good practice if you find that your mind wanders off into the future, thinking anxiously about things that you would do tomorrow or the day after tomorrow. When you surf the breath, there is only now.

Movement as a Portable Joy Locator

The human species is, by nature, an itinerant one. Movement from one continent to another has defined humanity's ability to explore and survive. Even in our modern times, when the need for physical activity has been reduced, movement plays an important role in achieving balance, well-being, and joy. Exercise has often been the subject of maintaining heart health and weight, but there are other forms of movement for finding a compass setting of true joy.

Tai chi is a form of exercise that dates back to thirteenth-century China. It is a method of gentle, very slow movement designed to support improved posture and balance, mental focus on the present moment, flexibility, and relaxation. It is a full body and mind practice that is both grounding and dynamic. A comprehensive review of literature on the therapeutic benefits of tai chi (Klein and Adams 2004) examined controlled clinical trials that met high experimental standards. The authors concluded that there are many clinical benefits to practicing tai chi, including better pain management, increased ability to tolerate physical activity, improved cardiovascular function, enhanced immune-system response, greater strength and flexibility, and overall improvement in the quality of life. The real benefit of a tai chi practice, or other deliberate movement practices—yoga, qigong, and mindful walking—is that motion itself becomes a meditation. By getting fully embodied, we enter present-moment time.

Walking is another ideal practice for getting grounded. It's ideal because we use it so frequently. Whether walking to or from the car or between rooms, we have the opportunity to use our joy compass simply by taking a few steps. But to do so requires a very different approach from that usually taken while walking—which is to be out of the body and let the body's automatic-movement centers take over. Yes, that means that we can walk, talk, and chew gum at the same time. But it also means that while your body is moving forward, it may actually be forgotten and left behind. What follows is a practice that is much like tai chi but is focused on getting grounded in the practice of full-presence walking.

Walking with full presence means going off autopilot. It means stepping in order to take a step, lifting your foot in order to lift it, pivoting your leg through the air in order to pivot it, shifting your weight from one side of the body to the other in order to shift the weight. There is nothing accidental in full-presence walking. While you may be walking toward a particular place, that is not the purpose here. Neither is speed. Your only purpose is to take that next step with complete awareness. So long as your body is pointed in the right direction, you can be assured that you will reach your destination.

Practice: Full-Presence Walking

After reading through these instructions, practice full-presence walking for approximately one to five minutes—although you can always go for longer if you want—bringing all your attention to every movement.

In order to experience full-presence walking, bring your awareness into your entire body, much as you did with the surfing the breath practice. This shift means that it is not your body that is doing the walking, but your entire awareness. Take the following three steps:

1. Find a quiet place where you can take ten to twenty steps. You will be moving slowly, so you may want to be near a wall to steady yourself if necessary.

2. Stand and become aware of your whole body. You can surf the breath while standing to help you get into the body. Feel the soles of your feet grounded to the floor and the earth. Allow your body to naturally find its balance,

rooted firmly and securely. Notice your posture. Let your body adjust in order to assume a dignified and graceful posture.

3. Move slowly, deliberately, and with full awareness, as you take each step with the grace and dignity of a trained dancer. Moving lightly, walk peacefully, not harshly or thoughtlessly, through your space. In this same way, you can move through your day—with care, balance, and full attention. Your body continues to move, without wasting thought or movement on anything else. This is sustainable walking, a means of learning how to do anything sustainably.

If, at any time, your mind leaves your body because of a distraction—because of a thought or a sensation that attracts the mind—simply return your presence to each movement and step. Be aware of your breath as you move, but you needn't synchronize your breathing with your steps.

Continue to walk in this way, feeling the joy of how your body moves and follows your every command. Don't worry about how slowly or quickly you are walking, so long as your awareness is walking with you.

Reflections on Full-Presence Walking

How did it feel to focus on the journey, experiencing each step, instead of focusing on the destination? How hard or easy was it for you to bring awareness into your feet, your legs, and your arms? Did you notice how each step was unique? What was it like to balance when walking in this way?

Do you have greater appreciation for how the body coordinates its movements? Do you recognize how miraculous each step can be?

Perhaps the most valuable lesson of walking is that by fully embodying awareness, we can learn how to be more present with all things in our lives—rather than leave for somewhere else. How can stepping more gently, deliberately, and sustainably reverberate in other areas of your life?

Experiment with the speed of full-presence walking. You can try it very slowly, at a normal pace, and at a brisk pace. There is no correct speed, so long as you are walking with full presence.

Full-Body Grounding to Enhance Your Well-Being

One systematic method of training the mind to focus on the whole body is known as mindfulness-based stress reduction (MBSR). This is a means for getting out of your head and into your body by paying attention in a nonjudgmental way to whatever is occurring—moment by moment. This approach to grounding, developed by Jon Kabat-Zinn and adapted from Buddhist practice, has been tested across many different populations and contexts. A meta-analysis (Grossman et al. 2004) reviewed studies meeting high empirical criteria that covered a wide range of clinical populations, including people with cancer, pain, heart disease, anxiety, and depression. Also included were nonclinical groups dealing with high stress. The study concluded that MBSR had benefits ranging from helping people cope with daily stress to improving quality of life and reducing pain for people with more serious conditions.

MBSR was even found beneficial for a group of adolescent boys (Huppert and Johnson 2010). In this study, the boys practiced for only forty minutes once a week in class for four consecutive weeks, after which time they were found to display increased positive emotions, interest, and contentment. Boys who had the highest levels of anxiety benefited the most from the practice. Those who practiced more frequently at home also showed greater improvement. These studies illustrate how MBSR effectively sets your joy compass in ways that can make an impact and enhance feelings of well-being—regardless of age.

As a psychotherapist, I have witnessed how a full-body grounding practice has helped clients get centered. One former methamphetamine addict whom I worked with used this practice every day to powerfully get in the moment and turn away from cravings. Another client, who struggled with chronic pain, used this practice to change how she experienced pain. Yet another found that this practice helped lessen depressive and anxious thoughts when used first thing in the morning. Many clients just liked it because it helped them arrive at that more serene and less anxious place known as the here and now. Try this practice and see how you can adapt it to help you find joy.

Practice: Surfing the Body

The traditional body scan, which I learned while in the monastery, brings full attention to each part of your body—one part at a time. The way I like to teach this practice is to ask you to start at the left foot and slowly surf up the left side of the body with your awareness. When you reach your head, you can then surf down the right side until you end up at the right foot. In this way, surfing the body is very easy to remember.

Here are some useful guidelines:

1. Surf each part of the body in an open and neutral way. Allow yourself to deeply experience your whole foot, including the surface of the skin, the deep tissue, the ligaments, the bones, and the tendons. Your complete awareness surfs along with whatever sensation arises in this new moment and the next new one and the next. Just notice feelings for what they are, even before the mind can give them a name. Continually let go of sensations so that you can make space for the next one—and the next.

2. Allow your consciousness to flow freely as you surf from one part of the body to the next. Optionally, you can surf several parts at the same time, such as the lower leg, the upper leg, the arm, the neck and shoulders, and so on. Don't forget to surf the inner organs, like the stomach, liver, kidneys, heart, and lungs. When you get to the face, you can sense individual parts, like the lips, cheeks, nose, eyes, chin, scalp, and so on.

   For your first surfing session, I recommend surfing up one side of your body and down the other. Stop for prolonged surfing wherever it feels natural.

3. If your mind travels elsewhere, just gently bring it back to the body. If, for any reason (trauma or pain), you find it too hard to be in the body, quit the surfing process. You are

always in charge. If this is really difficult for you because of past trauma, you may want to consider getting professional help. You can also limit surfing to one innocuous part of your body, such as the tip of your pinky finger.

4. Surf for as long as you want—from a few seconds to a few minutes—on each part of your body. Don't be too quick to hurry away if you don't immediately notice a sensation. You don't have to wiggle your toes or do something to create a sensation. Just rest and settle in. Your body is naturally dynamic, and you will start to notice sensations, given enough time and patience.

5. Don't worry about timing yourself when you try this practice. Instead, just note what time you started and finished, and figure out how much time passed. Eventually, you will develop a routine and get a sense of how much time it takes for you to experience dropping into the body.

After you get comfortable with these guidelines, start the practice.

Reflections on Surfing the Body

How well did surfing the body ground you? How can you adapt this practice to your day or lifestyle? How will it be valuable for you? What is the greatest challenge to doing this practice: finding time, finding a quiet place? You don't, for example, have to surf the entire body each time you practice.

It's also worth paying attention to how moment-by-moment sensations in the body differ from the narrative story you may have around a bodily pain or a judgment you have about the body. While these things are connected, the sensation is not the story. How can body surfing create space from a painful body story—thus altering your relationship to a pain or trauma?

Practice: Instant Grounding with BE-THIS

I have designed an instant grounding method that goes by the acronym BE-THIS. The advantage to this practice is that you can quickly use it anywhere: while stuck in a traffic jam, before an anxiety-inducing interview, when dealing with a craving, and any time you need to quickly get grounded in the body.

If you spend an average of just fifteen seconds on each step, you will be grounded in about one and a half minutes. The more you practice, the better results you will get. Now, follow each of these steps:

1. *B* = Breathe (10 seconds): Take two deeply satisfying belly breaths.

2. *E* = Emotion (20 seconds):

    a. Sense the location of tightness or emotion in your body.

    b. Visualize your next in-breath traveling to the part of the body filled with the tension or emotion. Let the breath absorb all the impurities, as you…

    c. Exhale, letting the breath carry all negative tension out the soles of your feet and harmlessly depositing them back into the earth.

3. *T* = Touch (15 seconds): Use your fingers to explore a nearby object (keys, pen, book, cup, shirt, and so forth) in great detail. Notice the weight, temperature (hot, cold, warm), texture, color, material, symmetry, and shape. Allow yourself to appreciate how each item is the product of much effort, energy, and nature.

4. *H* = Hear (15 seconds): Pay close attention to the moment-by-moment sounds around you, from the most subtle and soft to the loudest. You may even notice the sounds of your own breath. Let go of each sound to hear the next, without judgment.

5. *I* = Intentional movement (15 seconds): Set an intention to make a satisfying and stress-releasing movement, such as rolling your shoulders several times, stretching your arms up high over your head, or releasing neck tension by rolling your head in a circle a few times.

6. *S* = Sight and Smell (15 seconds): Use your senses of sight and smell to notice all the pleasant things you can find around you. What favorite colors or objects do you see? If you are looking outside, notice the weather. What is the aroma of the place?

Reflections on Instant Grounding with BE-THIS

What was it like to get grounded in only 90 seconds? How did this practice help you move away from the past and future to find joy in the little things before you? How can you start a BE-THIS practice so that you can get grounded anytime, anywhere? When do you think this joy-locating practice would be most useful?

CHAPTER 10

Thrive through Love and Social Connections

Would you knowingly partake in a behavior that was proven to shorten your life as much as smoking fifteen cigarettes a day does? How about starting a behavior whose negative effect on your life span was equivalent to that of being an alcoholic? How ready would you be to engage in an activity that was twice as harmful to your health as obesity? Believe it or not, a single behavior has been shown to shorten life expectancy as significantly as smoking, alcoholism, and obesity. This culprit not only dampens joy, but also considerably diminishes the amount of time you may have to experience it. The activity that is responsible is this: isolation from others.

The Benefits of Connecting with Others

A team of researchers at Brigham Young University found that people who had a strong social network enjoyed a 50 percent greater chance of living longer than those who were isolated and didn't have good support. The study (Holt-Lunstad, Smith, and Layton 2010) was a meta-analysis that examined more than 148 studies that included over 300,000 participants. The results of having social support were dramatic, and according to the study, social connections had a greater positive impact on preventive health care than taking drugs to control high blood pressure or even getting a vaccine to prevent pneumonia.

Interestingly, the researchers also found that Americans had become increasingly more isolated over the previous two decades. They found that the number of people reporting a lack of loving relationship and a supportive confidant had tripled. What's more, adults are not the only ones experiencing this loss. We need to support a generation of children who are increasingly isolated due to technology overuse. Web-based social networking sites may provide some sense of connection, but they may also keep individuals from having face-to-face interactions that are the key to unlocking deeper sustenance and locating joy.

One factor in the harmful effect of isolation may be cortisol. This is a stress hormone that doesn't exactly locate joy. One study (Adam et al. 2006) found a link between loneliness and cortisol. In fact, it found that individuals who went to bed after a day of feeling angry and lonely woke up in the morning with elevated levels of cortisol. It was as if their bodies were preparing these people for yet another stressful day. Fortunately, it doesn't have to be that way.

It's important to recognize that a social network can come in many different shapes and sizes. When Bob came to me for help, he shared a life story filled with difficulties ranging from substance abuse to membership in a gang. His family was severely dysfunctional, and support was practically nonexistent. But despite having spent much of his adult life in and out of prison, Bob was determined to turn his life around one step at a time. The reason for Bob's visit was clear: having returned to school at the age of thirty-eight, it looked as if a community college training program was going to do him in. He was failing his classes and was highly distracted by personal issues. Bob needed to identify resources to help him navigate this new life path.

After I asked Bob some questions, it became clear that he had no idea how to manage his study time. I suggested that he find a resource person at the college who could help him craft a daily study schedule. When Bob returned the following week, he proudly showed me a study spreadsheet that detailed his study time for each week of the term. "I started asking around," he said, "and someone told me about this posting on a bulletin board. So I called, and they worked out a complete schedule. Now I know what I have to do each day." My work with Bob also included helping him manage his stress and find other supportive resources.

Another client, fifty-five-year-old Beverly, had cared for her aging parents for several years. While this had been extremely important to her, she had become so immersed in her parents' final years that she had lost all touch with her own social network. By the time Beverly came to see me, four years after the death of her parents, she was still grieving and isolating herself from others. Part of her grief, I believe, was due to the fact that her social network had consisted solely of her parents and their caregivers. Instead of building a new network—such as with coworkers in the office where she worked—she kept to herself and dwelled on the past.

To get Beverly connecting again with others, I encouraged her to seek out connections in her workplace, as well as make a list of all the activities that could help her transition from a grieving place into the social realm. Eventually, she started tapping into the myriad of joyful social activities she had always found sustaining, such as dancing, yoga, going to church, and meeting with others over a meal.

As these examples point out, your joy compass can get activated from many sources other than family or friends. You can also find immense joy in having pets. Activities and professional support are another important avenue for finding joy. The following practice will point out the different areas from which you can gain and sustain social connections.

Practice: Daily Time Spent with Others

How isolated or connected are you? How much time do you spend face to face with significant others in your life? This practice will help you track how isolated or connected you are.

For the next week, do your best to track the amount of uninterrupted time you spend with others, as well as the time you spend alone. It can also be useful to track the amount of time you spend with electronic technology, not interacting face to face with others. To get the average amount of time, track the following categories on a daily basis:

- Uninterrupted time spent in person with significant others (at home)
- Time spent alone with technology (at home)
- Uninterrupted time spent in person with others (at work)
- Time spent alone with technology (at work)
- Uninterrupted time spent in person with others (outside home)

Reflections on Daily Time Spent with Others

Were you surprised by the results of your exploration? Are you spending less time than you would like with significant others in your life? What would it be like if you could increase quality time with others? What adjustments would you like to make about how you interact with others or with technology? What would be the challenges you would face? What is one small change that you could make right now?

Remember, the purpose of this practice is not to avoid technology, but to find a meaningful and joyful balance between the dynamics of technology and social activity.

Practice: Identifying Resources

On a sheet of paper, write down the following six categories and make a corresponding list for each:

- *Family:* Make a list of family members who are supportive of you, regardless of their proximity to you. Don't forget to include extended family who may have special work expertise or other talents that you can draw on.
- *Friends/Associates:* A supportive friend or associate doesn't have to be your "BFF," best friend forever! For example, even having a neighbor whom you can have a brief, pleasant exchange with is an important joy connection.
- *School/Workplace:* Locate people at your school or workplace who make you laugh. Take the time to learn about the full range of supportive resources that are available to you—from counselors to human-resources professionals.
- *Activities:* Don't be shy or modest when creating a list of activities or classes you might want to try, such as yoga, meditation, dancing, music, sports, swimming, art, tai chi, book clubs, volunteering, and others. You don't have to be Picasso to take an art class; you don't have to be a sports star to join a softball league. Also, if you have taken part in an activity in the past, write it down anyway. You may find that reconnecting with an old hobby is like trying on a comfortable, favorite pair of shoes.
- *Caregivers/Professionals/Self-Help:* There are a host of people available to support your emotional and physical well-being, including doctors, dentists, mental health

professionals, acupuncturists, chiropractors, dietitians, naturopaths, life coaches, exercise trainers, 12-step programs, women's groups, men's groups, telephone hotline operators, and online support groups.

- *Church/Religious/Spiritual:* There are philosophy clubs and groups that explore meaning for almost every persuasion, from religious and humanist to pantheist and atheist. Conversations about living a life that matters can help you locate like-minded individuals whose values match your own.

Reflections on Identifying Resources

What did you discover by creating a list of support systems? Did you find more than you had imagined? What are the ones that you can start using right away? Which ones will take time to cultivate? Which ones get your joy compass working quickly?

Most important, what is one small, realistic, and achievable step you can take, either today or this week, to make a satisfying connection with another person? How would this action enhance your life, your mood, and your ability to experience joy?

Enhance Your Relationships

While a number of relationship studies investigate stressed-out or at-risk couples, one study (Carson et al. 2004) took the unique approach of using mindfulness training with couples who were already well adjusted and fairly happy. The purpose was to see whether such practices as meditation, yoga, mindfulness, awareness of emotions, and a welcoming openness toward your partner could enrich an already solid relationship. Couples were trained in eight weekly sessions lasting two and a half hours and received one daylong training. Couples filled out a daily diary that tracked such items as relationship happiness, relationship stress, and how well they were coping. The results showed that couples who had trained in mindfulness were better able to cope with relationship stress and felt increased optimism, closeness, and acceptance.

One of the qualities of mindfulness is that it invites a sense of curiosity to each interaction. To take a mindfulness approach with another person, even someone you have known for years, is to experience that person as if the two of you had just met. It means suspending and letting go of any attitude of judgment, dread, or boredom that arises. Russian novelist Leo Tolstoy (2009) wrote a short parable, "Three Questions," which sheds light on this more expansive way of relating to others in the moment. The story is about the search for the answer to three apparently simple questions: What is the most important time? Who are the most important people? What is the most important thing to do?

The wise man in the story explains that the most important time is now, the most important person is whoever happens to be at your side in this moment, and the most important thing to do is show compassion and caring. Not only is this Tolstoy's joy compass in three questions—but it is also a method for extending happiness to others.

Practice: Being Open and Present with Another Person

How present are you when you are with another person? In this practice you will focus on being present, open, and accepting. The next time you meet or greet someone—a new acquaintance or an old friend—try these four straightforward strategies.

- *Release your assumptions.* What assumptions, beliefs, or opinions do you hold about this person? How are these preconceptions getting in the way? Allow yourself to let go of your assumptions for one minute at a time so that you can experience the unique person before you in a fresh and accepting way.
- *Listen with respect.* Know that deep down, each person wants to be respected and appreciated. Listen without interrupting, show interest, and maintain calm and non-threatening body language.
- *Be curious.* Take the approach that this person has experiences to share with you. With a curious mind-set, ask questions and get clarification. Seek out new meaning, new ideas, and new information.
- *Make yourself available.* Think of what you have to offer this person and how that compassion will enhance the relationship. This might mean going out of your comfort zone, and it could include asking how you could be of assistance.

Reflections on Being Open and Present with Another Person

Before you even get the chance to use the four guidelines just introduced, what do you think this will be like? Have opinions and judgment made it difficult for you to connect with others? Have you seen how judging others can harm your relationships? Can you let go of assumptions when another person is opinionated? What do you think it will be like to make yourself more available than you perhaps have been in the past? Even bringing these questions into your awareness can help you move in the direction of becoming more available.

After you have had the opportunity to actually put these four guidelines into action, contemplate the following questions: *How did dropping my own assumptions allow me to be more present? How did showing respect and acknowledging another's need to be heard change the interaction? What did I learn about the other person that surprised me? How did it feel to make myself available in some way?* Be patient with yourself as you practice these four guidelines for being open, present, and accepting. Continue to use these guidelines to unlock the vast potential of joy that is waiting in your next encounter.

Share Your Joy

Have you ever known people who constantly served up large helpings of their suffering, unable to see the positive things that life had to offer? Maybe you have encountered someone who couldn't give you the supportive words you always craved.

Or, perhaps you know someone who is constantly irritated and annoyed by little things. If any of these describes you, then it proves that you are only human. After all, each of us is vulnerable to these behaviors and reactions.

Whether you have been on the giving or receiving end of a rant, what better starting point is there from which to cultivate a new attitude of joy for others? Besides, an occasional rant may be healthy, so long as it doesn't block out the rest of your view. However, in the long term, it's sharing your joy that will build relationships that are endearing and enduring.

One study (Mauss et al. 2011) that investigated the effects of sharing happiness on social connectedness found that letting others know about your positive feelings enhanced connections with others. Signaling positive feelings also helped improve psychological functioning, or sense of well-being. In addition, researchers found that a positive signal, such as a smile, needed to be authentic in order to strengthen the connection. If the expressed feeling was not genuine, then it impeded both a sense of closeness and well-being.

Expressing joyfulness for others has a long history. In Buddhism, for example, *mudita*, or sympathy of joy, is considered one of the heavenly abodes: a noble, dignified, and highly regarded way of expressing joyfulness for others. This means that you celebrate and support the joyfulness of another person, even if you don't happen to agree with that person's path or direction. This is the flip side of compassion, in which you are present with another person's suffering.

Sharing your own joy with others is important, too. This doesn't mean gloating; rather, it means lending hope and optimism to others through sharing the stories of your success and happiness. Instead of spreading the emotional contagion of negativity, you can help someone catch the sweetness of life and locate joy in the process. How empowering!

Practice: A Personal Joy Journal

Each day, track the two different forms of joy:

- Sharing your joy instead of your pain
- Sharing joyousness for the victories of others

Write down all the examples of each type of joy that you partake in. Also, remember to write down how your joy-sharing made you feel in the moment and afterward.

Optionally, you can take two small teacups and label them "Sharing My Joy" and "Joy for Others." Put a penny in each cup for every time that you did your practice. See how many pennies you can accumulate by the end of a week.

Reflections on a Personal Joy Journal

After you have had the opportunity to practice, ask yourself: *How did sharing my joy with others make me feel? Did I feel elevated, happy, expansive, or giving? Did I smile, laugh, or give a hug? Did my joy enhance the closeness of my relationships?*

Likewise, how did supporting the joy of others make you feel? There are always decisions made by parents, children, friends, or others that leave you scratching your head—or worse. Did you find it difficult to show joy when you didn't fully agree with another person's decision? How did you manage to overcome your internal judgments? You can always remind yourself of the times you did something that another person disapproved of. Maybe you learned a valuable lesson from your choice, or maybe you wish you had been more supportive of others. Either way, you are embarking on a new path to build relationships and love—and that makes the journey worthwhile.

As you continue using your joy compass as a trusted guide, don't stop looking for new ways to enhance this unfolding moment. The eight joy pathways in this book—laughter, gratitude, forgiveness, music, contemplation, affirmations, the here and now, and social connections—are more than enough to keep your joy compass working for a long, long time. May you continue to discover and manifest the joy and the peace within so that they may manifest in all beings.

Resources for Continuing Your Journey to Joy

Congratulations on your efforts to find joy. You will find further helpful information at my websites: *The Joy Compass* (thejoycompass.com), *One-Minute Mindfulness* (oneminute mindfulnessbook.com), *Mindful Practices for Living: Creative Healing and Self-Enrichment* (mindfulpractices.com), and *The Mindfulness Code* (mindfulnesscode.com).

There are many other resources for connecting to joy. Listed here are various organizations that bring joy seekers together, as well as further the quest for meaning, peace, and deepening awareness.

A Campaign for Forgiveness Research, a site that promotes forgiveness by including scientific forgiveness research from around the world: forgiving.org.

A Network for Grateful Living, a nonprofit organization whose mission is to provide gratitude resources and promote the power of grateful living: www.gratefulness.org.

CANDLES Holocaust Museum, a museum dedicated to children of the Holocaust, founded by Eva Kor, that promotes forgiveness and understanding through stories, teaching, and resources: candlesholocaustmuseum.org.

The Center for Contemplative Mind in Society, a nonprofit organization that promotes contemplative practices from all traditions through training and resources: contemplativemind.org.

The Center for Mindful Eating, a nonprofit organization dedicated to providing mindful eating training and support to professionals and others: tcme.org.

Center for Mindfulness in Medicine, Health Care, and Society, a leader in the field of mind-body medicine that promotes research and integration of mindfulness into medicine and the mainstream: umassmed.edu/content.aspx?id=41252.

The Dana Foundation, publisher of newsletters and updates on advances in brain research: dana.org.

The Forgiveness Project, an organization dedicated to promoting nonviolent means of resolving conflict that provides healing stories of forgiveness, including outreach and education: theforgivenessproject.com.

Lab for Affective Neuroscience, a research and education center for exploring the brain mechanisms underlying emotion and emotion regulation: psyphz.psych.wisc.edu.

Laughter Heals Foundation, a nonprofit organization with the mission of increasing awareness of laughter that supports its use in the world of health care: laughterheals.org.

Laughter Yoga International, a form of yoga, founded by Dr. Madan and Madhuri Kataria, that combines laughter with movement and now features hundreds of laughter clubs around the world: laughteryoga.org.

Music and Happiness, a site created by two musicians with articles and resources about the power of music to uplift and heal: musicandhappiness.com.

Optimist International, an association of more than 2,900 clubs around the world dedicated to helping children, with adults who join participating in leading positive service projects: optimist.org.

UCLA Mindful Awareness Research Center, an organization that strives to promote mindful awareness across the life span by providing education and resources: marc.ucla.edu.

References

Adam, E. K., L. C. Hawkley, B. M. Kudielka, and J. T. Cacioppo. 2006. "Day-to-Day Dynamics of Experience: Cortisol Associations in a Population-Based Sample of Older Adults." *Proceedings of the National Academy of Sciences of the United States of America* 103 (45):17058–63. doi:10.1073/pnas.0605053103.

American Institute of Physics 2008. "Music Went with Cave Art in Prehistoric Caves." *ScienceDaily*, July 4. Retrieved May 6, 2011. http://www.sciencedaily.com/releases/2008/07/080704130439.htm.

American Physiological Society (APS). 2006. "Maybe Laughter Really Is the Best Medicine, and It's Prophylactic!" Retrieved November 30, 2011. http://the-aps.org/press/conference/eb06/10.htm.

Bartlett, M. Y., and D. DeSteno. 2006. "Gratitude and Prosocial Behavior: Helping When It Costs You." *Psychological Science* 17 (4):319–25.

Baum, L. F. 1900. *The Wonderful Wizard of Oz*. With illustrations by W. W. Denslow. Chicago: George M. Hill Company.

Bennett, M. P., J. M. Zeller, L. Rosenberg, and J. McCann. 2003. "The Effect of Mirthful Laughter on Stress and Natural Killer Cell Activity." *Alternative Therapies in Health and Medicine* 9 (2):38–45.

Bradt, S. 2010. "Wandering Mind Not a Happy Mind." *Harvard Gazette*, November 11. Harvard University. Retrieved May 16, 2011. http://news.harvard.edu/gazette/story/2010/11/wandering-mind-not-a-happy-mind/.

Carson, J. W., K. M. Carson, K. M. Gil, and D. H. Baucom. 2004. "Mindfulness-Based Relationship Enhancement." *Behavior Therapy* 35:471–94.

Carson, J. W., F. J. Keefe, V. Goli, A. M. Fras, T. R. Lynch, S. R. Thorp, and J. L. Buechler. 2005. "Forgiveness and Chronic Low Back Pain: A Preliminary Study Examining the Relationship of Forgiveness to Pain, Anger, and Psychological Distress." *Journal of Pain* 6 (2):84–91.

Carson, J. W., F. J. Keefe, T. R. Lynch, K. M. Carson, V. Goli, A. M. Fras, and S. R. Thorp. 2005. "Loving-Kindness Meditation for Chronic Low Back Pain: Results from a Pilot Trial." *Journal of Holistic Nursing* 23 (3):287–304.

Creswell, J. D., B. M. Way, N. I. Eisenberger, and M. D. Lieberman. 2007. "Neural Correlates of Dispositional Mindfulness during Affect Labeling." *Psychosomatic Medicine* 69 (6):560–65.

Davila Ross, M., S. Menzler, and E. Zimmermann. 2008. "Rapid Facial Mimicry in Orangutan Play." *Biology Letters* 4 (1):27–30.

Easwaran, E. 2009. *The Mantram Handbook: A Practical Guide to Choosing Your Mantram and Calming Your Mind.* Tomales, CA: Nilgiri Press.

Enright, R. D. 2001. *Forgiveness Is a Choice: A Step-By-Step Process for Resolving Anger and Restoring Hope*. Washington, DC: American Psychological Association LifeTools.

Goines, L., and L. Hagler. 2007. "Noise Pollution: A Modern Plague." *Southern Medical Journal* 100 (3):287–94.

Goldsman, A., and S. Nasar. 2001. A *Beautiful Mind*, film directed by R. Howard. Universal City, Glendale, and Beverly Hills, CA: Universal Pictures, DreamWorks SKG, and Imagine Entertainment respectively.

Grossman, P., L. Niemann, S. Schmidt, and H. Walach. 2004. "Mindfulness-Based Stress Reduction and Health Benefits: A Meta-Analysis." *Journal of Psychosomatic Research* 57 (1):35–43.

Holt-Lunstad, J., T. B. Smith, and J. B. Layton. 2010. "Social Relationships and Mortality Risk: A Meta-analytic Review." *Public Library of Science Medicine* 7 (7):e1000316. doi:10.1371/journal.pmed.1000316.

Huppert, F. A., and D. M. Johnson. 2010. "A Controlled Trial of Mindfulness Training in Schools: The Importance of Practice for an Impact on Well-Being." *Journal of Positive Psychology* 5 (4):264–74.

Jaffe, E. 2010. "This Side of Paradise: Discovering Why the Human Mind Needs Nature." *APS Observer* 23 (5):11–15.

Kahn, P. H., Jr., B. Friedman, B. Gill, J. Hagman, R. L. Severson, N. G. Freier, E. N. Feldman, S. Carrère, and A. Stolyar. 2008. "A Plasma Display Window? The Shifting Baseline Problem in a Technologically Mediated Natural World." *Journal of Environmental Psychology* 28:192–99.

Khurana, A., and P. L. Dhar. 2000. "Effect of Vipassana Meditation on Quality of Life, Subjective Well-Being, and Criminal Propensity among Inmates of Tihar Jail, Delhi."

Vipassana Research Institute, June. Retrieved November 16, 2011. http://www.vridhamma.org/Research-on-inmates-of-Tihar-Jail-Delhi.

Killingsworth, M. A., and D. T. Gilbert. 2010. "A Wandering Mind Is an Unhappy Mind." *Science* 330 (6006):932.

Klein, P. J., and W. D. Adams. 2004. "Comprehensive Therapeutic Benefits of Taiji: A Critical Review." *American Journal of Physical Medicine and Rehabilitation* 83 (9):735–45.

Levitin, D. J. 2008. *The World in Six Songs: How the Musical Brain Created Human Nature*. New York: Dutton.

Libet, B. 2004. *Mind Time: The Temporal Factor in Consciousness*. Cambridge, MA: Harvard University Press.

Lieberman, M. D., N. I. Eisenberger, M. J. Crockett, S. M. Tom, J. H. Pfeifer, and B. M. Way. 2007. "Putting Feelings into Words: Affect Labeling Disrupts Amygdala Activity in Response to Affective Stimuli." *Psychological Science* 18 (5):421–28.

Linley, A., J. Willars, and R. Biswas-Diener. 2010. *The Strengths Book: Be Confident, Be Successful, and Enjoy Better Relationships by Realising the Best of You*. Coventry, UK: CAPP Press.

Mauss, I. B., A. J. Shallcross, A. S. Troy, O. P. John, E. Ferrer, F. H. Wilhelm, and J. J. Gross. 2011. "Don't Hide Your Happiness! Positive Emotion Dissociation, Social Connectedness, and Psychological Functioning." *Journal of Personality and Social Psychology* 100 (4):738–48.

McCullough, M. E., R. A. Emmons, and J.-A. Tsang. 2002. "The Grateful Disposition: A Conceptual and Empirical Topography." *Journal of Personality and Social Psychology* 82 (1):112–27.

Mehl-Madrona, L. 2010. *Healing the Mind through the Power of Story: The Promise of Narrative Psychiatry*. Rochester, VT: Bear and Company.

Meijer, L. 1999. "Vipassana Meditation at the North Rehabilitation Facility." *American Jails*, July–August. Reprint retrieved November 16, 2011. http://www.prison.dhamma.org/AJart99.pdf.

Needleman, J. 2011. "The Wisdom of Atonement." In *Beyond Forgiveness: Reflections on Atonement*, edited by P. Cousineau, 19–34. San Francisco: Jossey-Bass.

Nilsson, U., N. Rawal, L. E. Uneståhl, C. Zetterberg, and M. Unosson. 2001. "Improved Recovery after Music and Therapeutic Suggestions during General Anaesthesia: A Double-Blind Randomised Controlled Trial." *Acta Anaesthesiologica Scandinavica* 45 (7):812–17.

O'Connor, R. 2005. *Undoing Perpetual Stress: The Missing Connection between Depression, Anxiety, and 21st Century Illness*. New York: Berkley Publishing Group.

Peden, A. R., M. K. Rayens, L. A. Hall, and L. H. Beebe. 2001. "Preventing Depression in High-Risk College Women: A Report of an 18-Month Follow-Up." *Journal of American College Health* 49 (6):299–306.

Sandgren, M. 2005. "Becoming and Being an Opera Singer: Health, Personality, and Skills." Doctoral dissertation. Faculty of Social Sciences, Department of Psychology, Stockholm University. URI:urn:nbn:se:su:diva-448. Retrieved October 23, 2011. http://urn.kb.se/resolve?urn=urn:nbn:se:su:diva-448.

Smith, E. R. 1993. *Falling Down*, film directed by J. Schumacher. Los Angeles: Alcor Films, Canal+, Regency Enterprises, Warner Bros. Pictures.

Teicher, M. H., J. A. Samson, A. Polcari, and C. E. McGreenery. 2006. "Sticks, Stones, and Hurtful Words: Relative Effects of Various Forms of Childhood Maltreatment." *American Journal of Psychiatry* 163 (6):993–1000. doi:10.1176/appi.ajp.163.6.993.

Tolstoy, L. 2009. *What Men Live By and Other Tales*. Rockville, MD: Wildside Press. First published 1918 by The Stratford Company, Boston, translated by L. and A. Maude.

Wolf, J. 2007. "Little Things Matter." *Parade*, December 16. Retrieved April 6, 2011. http://parade.com/articles/editions/2007/edition_12-16-2007/AOprah_and_Denzel.

Pavel G. Somov, PhD, is a licensed psychologist in private practice in Pittsburgh, PA. He is the author of *Eating the Moment*, *Present Perfect*, *The Smoke-Free Smoke Break*, and *The Lotus Effect*. Visit his online Mindful Eating Tracker at

www.eatingthemoment.com/mindfulness-tracker.

Foreword writer **Donald Altman, MA, LPC**, is vice president of The Center for Mindful Eating and author of *One-Minute Mindfulness* and *Meal by Meal*.